"The Nearly Man"

A TRUE STORY OF A YOUNG MAN'S STRIVING TO ACHIEVE HIS LIFE'S AMBITIONS AND FALLING JUST SHORT.

J.S.Nearey

Publishing Information

The Nearly Man.

This autobiography by author J.S.Nearey is published by Amazon Books [self publishing section].

The Title number: 4420172.

It can be ordered online via Amazon Books at:
http://www.amazon.com

Go onto: www.amazon.com, search into the "Book" section and look for: "The Nearly Man" ref: 4420172 or type in "The Nearly Man"

Version 2. Dated 5th.November 2013.

Contents

About the author   Page   5
Introduction   Page   8

Chapter	Page	
1	12	The Formative years
2	18	School days
3	40	Erdington Abbey
4	56	Mixing with the Parish
5	60	The Confessional
6	66	Matron
7	70	Junior Education
8.	76	Holidays at Home
9	86	Decision Time
10	90	Sixth Form
11	100	The Noviciate
12	106	Day One as a Novice
13	114	First Full Day
14	150	Decision Time
15	158	Moving On
16	170	New Dawn
17	184	The Redemptorist Way
18	190	Life at Hawkstone.
19	204	The Downward Spiral
20	258	The Final Solution

About the Author

Stephen Nearey was born on 17th.September 1948, at precisely 11.20am by his Mother Lily, in Crumpsall Hospital Manchester. His Father, Arthur Thomas Nearey, was at work at A.V.Roe, Lancaster Bomber Aircraft Manufacturers, at Woodford in Cheshire, where he worked as a Fitter. Rumour has it, that at 11.20 a.m. the precise time of Stephen's birth, that the factory horn sounded three times to announce the end of a tea break. His Dad, Arthur, had a rather different take on the horn sounding, preferring to believe that the triple blast of the horn was in honour of his 2nd son's birth.

This is the story of a young boy and young man, one and the same person. He was an unremarkable man, who lived the earlier part of his life and into young manhood and came very close to achieving a remarkable life's ambition.

From the tender age of just eleven years, with the help and encouragement of his parents and elder brother, he strived to become a member of a Religious Order; his crowning ambition was for him to become a Monk and a Missionary Priest of the Redemptorist Order.

The following pages describe the young life-story, of not just of one young man, but also a fitting commentary on the life and times of post war Catholics, attitudes to religion and life in general in the early 1960s, which were a time of major change and upheaval.

Stephen was never an avid reader of books, and he is to this day ashamed that until he produced this manuscript, he had not read a book in well over thirty years. All the more amazing then, that in his mid sixties, he has now put pen to paper, or at least key to keyboard, and wishes to tell the intriguing tale of his early life against the background of massive social change, new attitudes to religion and life, and it's interpretation of the truths which were held so absolutely and definitely, by most Catholics.

Stephen wishes to dedicate his book especially to his late Mother Lily, who passed away three years ago. Lily was the main driving force and mentor to Stephen in his early years and he would not have been able to achieve what he has in life without her encouragement, dedication, and sheer hard work, which paid for his school seminary fees. He also wishes to dedicate the book to his late Father, Arthur Thomas, and his elder brother, Arthur Charles, both of whom he held as great role models. Thanks also go to Keith Daniel who initially inspired Stephen to document this stage of his life. And, finally, and most importantly, Stephen dedicates the manuscript to his wonderful wife Anne, without who's total life support, this book would never have materialised.

That Stephen ultimately failed to achieve his main life's ambition is now a matter of fact. Yet he now holds his memories of those difficult years with some happiness, much sadness, but also a deep and lasting affection for those who helped to shape him into the person that he is today, whether that be good, bad or indifferent.

Stephen's desire to tell his story was borne out of a wish to explain to family, friends and anybody who reads it, about his past life, and the reasons why he followed this unusual lifestyle. It will perhaps explain to those who know him, just why he is the person he is today and the affect that it will have had on him as an adult person. It lays bare his soul and exposes not just his personality traits, but also his faults and weaknesses. As such, it has not been easy to write and publish this book and he pondered both long and hard before deciding to do so.

The author has no desire to make any monetary gain from this publication. It is sufficient for readers to enjoy the book and to understand the motives of the author. Instead, he wishes to assist a cause very close to his heart. Therefore, all Royalties earned by the publication of this book will go directly to Cancer Research UK.

The Author
J.S.Nearey

Introduction

I was on holiday in my Motor-home in 2010 and was speaking to a friend of mine, Keith Daniel, over a drink or two. As frequently happens, the subject eventually turned to politics and once we had done that topic to death, or even fallen out about it, the conversation moved onto religion and the meaning of life. At some point, the same question was always asked: "Do you actually believe in God?" Very few people have no view on it, and people rarely do not have an opinion on it at all. I have always held the view that a man would be foolish not to even consider the possibility that there may be a God. The fact is that no-one absolutely knows for sure that there is an almighty being that created this universe, as there is no definitive proof either way. It is all a matter of belief, and one day each of us will either know the answer for certain, or we will know nothing.

Whilst the four of us were giving our various "drink fuelled" opinions on such matters, the conversation came around to my own unusual background and upbringing. I usually find that people are fascinated to hear of my experiences as they appear to come from a different age, another moment in time; so unusual was the life of a Monastic. Keith was particularly interested in my upbringing without really giving any opinion about it at all, but what he did say started me thinking. He said: Steve *"There's a book in you somewhere!!* Eventually, after almost three years of insomnia, it has come to print.
Although I had considered such an option on more than

one occasion, I had not been motivated to do anything about it until that moment. Maybe I believed that nobody would ever be interested in reading about a story of my failed adventure. Perhaps I would be incapable of writing it? And yet, people I knew and met were always fascinated in listening to what I had to say, at least on this subject. Also, I had always been quite good at English, and English Literature, so perhaps after all, I may be able to write a book that would be passably readable?

When I was in my teens and twenties I was a good reader. I loved novels and I enjoyed reading biography. But then something went wrong and I know not why! I stopped reading books and although I was still a keen reader of periodicals, letters and newspapers, I could not bring myself to sit and read a book. I have been told by my wife, that it is because I do not know how to relax, and there is some merit in that opinion. So, I must have surprised myself, as well as those who know me, when I decided, on Keith's prompting, to write this book.

This is not just any book. It is perhaps the only book I could write, and there may never be another. It has been a difficult book to write, because it is a true story and it also highlights many of my own weaknesses and failings for the whole world to see. [Well perhaps not the entire world!]. I lay myself bare, for the world to dissect. This is not meant to be a masterpiece, a work of art, it is a simple story of the early life of a certain Stephen Nearey, and the life, times and social attitudes of Catholics in the 1950's and 1960's, many of whom were known to me.

It has also been difficult to write, because I could find no motivation in putting pen to paper during the day time. It was just as well then that during the winter of 2010, that I suffered a troublesome and lengthy bout of insomnia brought on by stress and anxiety. It was during these troubled periods when I could not sleep, that the story slowly began to unfold and take shape. I would sit in my office during the "wee small hours" of the morning and tap away on my computer. Even then, progress would be painfully slow. To make matters worse, my insomnia then improved, and I got better. I still did not write during daylight hours, but nor would I write at night, as I was then sleeping during the hours of darkness. In the end, it was just sheer determination to finish the project and to let it see the light of day that drove me to finish the manuscript. I had started writing in the autumn of 2010 and now drawing towards the autumn of 2013, the end is in sight. I hope that you will find the document to be both interesting and [in parts] amusing, and that it will enlighten you with regard to my early life story and a much wider understanding of what we Catholics were all about in the nineteen fifties, sixties and early seventies.

I wish to make it clear that everything I have written is the absolute truth, in my view, and to the best of my knowledge. If any of the material facts can be disputed, then it is because time has dimmed the memory, some forty five years on, and mistakes are a possibility, for which I humbly apologise to you in advance.

I would also like you to be aware that the facts and stories as detailed in the book are the viewpoint of just one man. I have told them honestly and to the very best of my knowledge and belief. It is not my intention or desire to cause any offence, or upset, or embarrassment by anything that I have said or implied. Indeed, I have deliberately omitted certain facts and stories that I may have wanted to include, so as ensuring that I do not to offend or embarrass anybody in any way whatsoever. As a precaution, I have changed the names of certain people mentioned in this book in order to guard their privacy and or reputation.

I do hope and wish that you find my first ever book [and possibly my last] to be informative, interesting and also entertaining and that you enjoy reading it even more than I have enjoyed writing it.

J.S.Nearey.

One
The Formative Years

The year was 1953, and Mum and Dad had recently been informed that they had been granted a brand spanking new Council House on the recently built Langley Estate in Middleton, Manchester. The War was still fresh in everyone's mind and rationing had not long since ended. The Council rules were that couples had to have at least two children in order to qualify for a Council property, and so when I burst onto the scene on 17th.September 1948, our family qualified initially for a prefabricated home in Moston, just South of Manchester. These were very quickly built post-war dwellings, built in a matter of weeks in order to re-house the thousands whose homes may have been bombed during the war and those that had been displaced by it. However, when two became three and my little sister Kathy arrived two years later, our family qualified for a new house on the Langley estate. It was a lovely new housing estate, initially consisting of just two or three roads and surrounded by lush green fields around the Middleton countryside. It was a far cry from central Manchester which was just being re-built after the blitz and was still showing the horrible scars from the bombing during the Second World War years.

It was a fresh start for a new young family, and far enough away from the smog and the smoke that encircled the towns and cities in the North West of England. On our first journey to our new home, I have an early memory of the thick clogging smog on the bus journey from

Manchester to Middleton. "Smog" was a word made up from "smoke" and "fog." The journey was all of 4 miles, but the smog which built up due to the factory chimneys, was so thick that the bus has to crawl along its journey at about 5mph, as the driver struggled to see a few feet in front of the bus, as he inched along his route. After what seemed to be an eternity in the dark smog, we arrived in Middleton and as the bus went up the hill towards the Langley Estate, we rose above the fog and the sun appeared. We were now looking down on the gloom which encircled Manchester and the surrounding areas, littered with chimneys and factories which were still pumping out more dirt and fumes which would create the next smog. But for us, Langley was a bright new dawn; it was a new home, a new beginning, a new post war era full of optimism and hope.

The Nearey family was one of the first few to arrive at the new Langley Estate. The theme for the housing was the Lake District, with all the roads and streets being named after famous lakes and places. Ennerdale Road was to be ours, in house number 66. It was next to Windermere Road which wound itself around the estate. Compared with the cramped and damp "prefab" in Manchester, the new three bed roomed house was luxury indeed. It wasn't a palace, but to us, it was the next best thing. We even had a garden, front and rear although to be frank, it was just a load of rubble to start with and we had to do something to turn it into a useable garden. Not that Dad was ever a Gardner. He was too busy working to feed his family. He was an aircraft fitter at A.V.Roe & Son and he would leave home at 6.30 in he morning, often doing overtime until about 7pm and getting home at about 8 o'clock, just as we kids were ready to go to bed. During the war Dad was too old to fight, as he was 40 when he first married. He was a member of the Home Guard, doing his bit for the war, but thankfully not having to join the forces. Mum worked in a munitions factory, so they both did their share for the war effort as did most of the population in one form or another. Make no mistake, times were hard, at least for inner city dwellers, and most were poor, with nearly everyone in the same situation. Food rationing had only recently finished, but now that food and goods were coming back into the shops, very few people could really afford them. In the early 1950's, obesity was not a problem for many. Of course, in most school classes, there was always one "Billy Bunter", but not many! If you were fat, then you must have been one of the lucky ones that had plenty to eat. The post war generation was largely fit and lithe due to the available food. We had enough, but no more, and generally we were slim although not necessarily healthy. There were too many underlying health problems for that. Many people had a bad chest due to the smog, with industry pumping out poisons into the atmosphere daily. Of course, nearly everyone smoked, thus adding to the bad atmosphere they were breathing anyway. Mum had been told that she had to get away from the City because of the bad chest condition she had. Moving to Langley was a good move, health wise, but of course, as with most of that generation, she smoked quite heavily, thus adding to the problems she already had. In those days, people genuinely believed that smoking was "good for you". It settled the nerves. Of course the advertising conditioned them to really believe that.

As the size of Langley Estate grew, and the estate became quite large, a community grew and developed. Unlike today's society, where you can live for years next to a neighbour and never know them, the people in the 1950's and early 60's were a true society. They lived close to each other, worked together, went to the same schools and clubs, and the entire society and social life revolved around the community, schools and the workplace. Nearly everyone knew everyone else. Neighbours would pop into each other's houses for a chat. Yes, they would borrow things from each other, and help each other out, and yes, people actually left their doors open. Unlike today, where everything has to be locked, doors were mostly open and people looked out for each other. Many is the time that Mum would send me across the road to a neighbour to borrow a cup of sugar, or some jam or bread, which Mum would return when Dad was paid on Thursday. Sometimes I was sent to borrow five shillings for school dinners until Dad got paid. Housekeeping money often did not stretch to a full week and if you didn't have cash, and you didn't have money, then you didn't eat. There were no credit cards then! Quite often after payday, the food was good and we even had treats like fruit or occasional sweets and crisps, but towards the end of the working week, Mum would be scratching around trying to make the money stretch and the family menu became noticeably sparser. There was nothing wrong with bread and jam, but that could sometimes be our main meal, and although we loved bread and dripping, I feel sure that the nutritional value was not what it should have been, and most likely, it was not at all healthy. Yes, compared to today, times were indeed hard for most Town and City dwellers in England.

I remember the Christmas Eve of 1955. I was seven years old, and like all children I was so very excited about Christmas. But things were not going well in the Nearey household. Dad had just finished his shift at work and had been paid. He was hoping to be home about lunchtime because Mum hadn't done any Christmas shopping. How could she? She had no money. It was impossible to save and we lived from week to week, sometimes from day to day. Dad arrived home at about 2pm and sheepishly he told Mum that he had lost his wage packet. He had worked three evening's overtime to earn extra money for Christmas, and his wage packet was fatter than most weeks. Needless to say, the atmosphere at home was not a good one, but in desperation, Dad went to the telephone box at the end of Ennerdale Road and telephoned the Police. Would you believe it? Some kind person had picked up Dad's wage packet where he had dropped it, and handed it into the Police – completely untouched! Some kind person, some really honest person had rescued our Christmas that year. There then followed a quick dash to the Police Station, by Mum, Dad and all the kids. Mum collected Dad's wages, and it was then 3.30pm on Christmas Eve. Mum practically ran around all the shops. I think we got a Chicken that year, which was a rare treat. Then it was off to the fruit shop. We didn't often have fruit. It was a luxury that most people had very rarely. In fact, an apple and an orange were traditionally a key part of any child's Christmas stocking, a real treat, along with a bag of mixed nuts. I think Dad kept us busy in town, while Mum ran around the shops before closing time in order to buy us our presents for Christmas. Of course, we all believed [quite rightly], that it was Santa Claus that brought the presents!

And so, finally, the Nearey family Christmas of 1955 was rescued, but only just in the nick of time. The next morning, on Christmas Day, our stockings were filled and there was a pillow case at the end of each of the children's beds which were full of goodies. It was, after all, a very, very good Christmas and one to remember.

The only Christmas not to remember was when Mum was talking about Christmas to me at the beginning of December 1957. I was nine years old at the time and she was talking about what presents I would like for Christmas. She said to me. *"Of course, you know that there isn't a Father Christmas, Stephen? You know it's me and you Dad that bring your presents?"* I looked at her, paused and then still in shock I said: *"Yes of course I know, Mum!"* I didn't know it at all. Of course the older kids would say things at school, but I would take no notice. Of course I did not want to believe. The magic of Christmas was never quite the same again.

Two
School Days

To this day in 2010 I still have a hatred of schools. From my first traumatic day, at aged five years, until I finished my education at 22 years, I had an inner fear and disliking for the whole "school thing". I suppose I came from a generation when children stayed with Mum until the day they went to school. There were no nurseries, no play-schools, no pre-school education of any sort, unless you class children's TV in the fifties as education. It was nothing at all like the "Cee-Beebies" generation of hi-tech pre-school entertainment, thinly disguised as education. The highlight of the day on television was "The Wooden-Tops" or "Rag, Tag and Bobtail for 15 minutes each day.

My first day at school was a scary affair. The teachers were not kindly and they were very formal, rigid and authoritarian. Looking back, they were the people of their times. These were indeed austere days with the memory of the war [although not for me] very close by. We were told to stand in lines, to be quiet and only to move at the sound of a very trill whistle. Woe betides any child that spoke or moved until the whistle had blown. One minute we were playing merrily in the playground and then STOP! The whistle sounded! Children in every corner of the playground stopped in their tracks. Immediately the loud cacophony of noise ceased and children stood like statues, seemingly for an age. With the whistle in his mouth, the teacher scanned the playground with his searching eyes, looking for any sound of noise or movement and then with another trill sound of his confounded whistle, the children all over the playground walked quickly and in silence and stood in straight lines outside the school door. With one final blow of the whistle the children filed into the school, line by line. Given that the country had just endured seven years of war and much of the country was seemingly in military uniform, it is not surprising that even everyday activities, such as the schools, were run in a military fashion and with similar precision.

I attended St. Mary's Roman Catholic School on the Langley Estate near Middleton, Manchester. Our family was Roman Catholic. Dad was born into a Catholic Family, but Mum was Church of England, and when she agreed to marry my Father, she changed her religion and became a Catholic. It was expected then, that any Catholic boy should marry a Catholic Girl. If however, the girl to be married was not Catholic then the rules were that the non-Catholic must agree to bring the children up in the Catholic faith. However, Mum decided to change her religion, much to the disgust of her entire family who promptly cut her off from her own family of eleven other children and her parents. It was not the done thing to move religion across the "divide". Her family refused to attend her wedding, let alone sanction it, and thereafter they had nothing more to do with Mum until very much later in life when it was all, quite frankly, far too late to make any amends and to make a difference.

As a young boy, I had no real knowledge of these religious matters, but I was soon to learn. Today, in 2010, the tensions in society are all about ethnic background and race. Indeed, in the fifties, nor was it easy to be a Jew or indeed German and living in the UK. However, in 1953, the genuine tensions were religious ones. There was a deep seated divide between Catholics and Non-Catholics of every type. Catholics were viewed by many at that time to be somewhat fanatical and to live by entirely different rules to the "normal" Christians in the UK. It was at a really young age of five, that I first realised that I was "different". I was to be segregated from my play friends and was to go to a school exclusively for Catholics. This in itself was unusual and I found it very difficult to understand. Catholics were one of only a few faith religions in the UK that insisted on segregated education for its young people. The thinking behind this was that young Catholics would be educated in the Catholic faith [much like the Jewish religion], and that Catholics would inter-marry, thus ensuring that the pure Catholicism would continue without being watered down by other sectors of Christianity. It was divisive and difficult to live with.

Living on a new housing estate in the semi rural areas of Middleton, there were no Catholic schools in the immediate area, other than the new "Infant" school at Langley. This I attended until I became the age of about seven when I had to move to the Primary school. Unfortunately, the nearest Catholic Primary School was some five miles away in Manchester. The mid-1950's did not have such a thing as a "school-run". We walked to school normally, but as we had to travel to St. Malachy's school in Manchester, we were taken there by the "Sharrah" [Charabanc], yester-years version of the modern coach. We had to get up really early to walk to school in Langley and then we were "bussed" to Manchester on the coach. On my first day of school at St.Malachy's our bus was stoned by Protestants [non-catholic] kids, as we drove past their school to get to ours. It was a rude, and a scary introduction to the inter-religion tensions at that time. After a while, we got used to the abuse and indeed we even used to throw back the insults. We were known as the "Cat-licks" [Catholics] and they were known as the "Proddy-Dogs". [Protestants]. It was not very nice, but these were the tensions of the 1950's and I was soon to learn that this extended into everyday life for both children and adults. In those days, there were Catholic Football Clubs {Manchester United and Celtic] and protestant clubs [Glasgow Rangers and Everton] to name just a few. I can understand now just how ethnic minorities feel when they encounter segregation and abuse, but for a young child, it was difficult to understand.

After a while, a new Catholic School was built at Langley for primary children, and the long haul into Manchester was stopped. The new school was Saint Mary's, built, paid for and run by the Catholic community in the area. Although there were secular catholic teachers in the school, it was largely run and controlled by the Parish Priest and his curates, and the Nuns who also lived and worked in the parish. At the very top was Father Murphy, a giant of an Irish man, or so he seemed at the time. He had curates Father O'Connor and Father Walsh. Also running the school was an order of Nuns in the parish. The nuns were very strict disciplinarians, two of which come to mind. There was Sister Bernadette, the very strictest of them all, and then Sister Barbara who seemed more kindly. Much of the curriculum in the early days was about religion and life, more so than lessons. Each new school day would begin with assembly and prayers and Father Murphy would take no prisoners if he found out that a child and its parents had not been seen at Mass on the previous Sunday. The very presence of the priests and the nuns in the school rooms ensured that the education was not just about lessons. It was very much about good and bad, religious education and life-style. Our entire community revolved around the Church, the school, and its many social clubs and activities. It says a lot about the type of education that just a few things have stuck in my mind. I cannot forget being called into the headmistress's office. I had to wait outside, for what seemed an eternity, knowing that I was going to get a beating. And I wondered why? Well I cannot remember, but it was something quite trivial by today's standards. Maybe it was talking in class or not paying attention, but at various times I was hit hard on the palm of the hand and the knuckles by the teachers. The routine was three or six strokes dependant on the seriousness of the misdemeanour. At another time [I must have been really bad!]; I remember being thrashed by a cane on the backside by a teacher. The thing that stuck in my memory was the force with which the teacher administered the beating, and to today, I can still see the look of anger and determination by the teacher to make sure that the child cried as he punished him. It is very sad that my lasting memories of the school were not good ones. They were not about my playmates, or the good teachers, or the fun we had playing and learning. Instead, they were about the cruel things that happened. I feel sure that there must have been good times and there must have been many good people, but the over-riding memories are of the bad things that happened to me. I find it hard to remember the names of many teachers, but for very good reason I remember the name of one. It was a certain Mr. McGinty, an Irish Teacher. He was a strict disciplinarian and he would not hesitate to administer corporal punishment to young children for quite trivial matters. I was not a difficult child or pupil by any means, in-fact, I was one of the quieter children, but I clearly remember, aged nine, being called to the front of the class and being hit with really vicious strokes, several times, by the edge of a twelve inch ruler on the knuckles. He chose to hit children on the knuckles because it hurt a lot more than on the palm of the hand. I cannot forget what seemed like pleasure on his face as he hit me hard six times on the knuckles. To this day I remember his name and his face. I cannot forget it.

Although corporal punishment was the norm in those days, it was administered for the most trivial of offences. It is less than a life time ago, but if the same things happened today, the teachers would be prosecuted for assault and child abuse. Another occasion that is etched in my mind was when we were being taught by a supply teacher. He was what is known as a "Christian Brother". This was an order of catholic clergy who do not become priests, but serve in a religious order in other ways. On this occasion, I was sat at the back of the class. So, maybe I was not paying attention, and I should have been, but the Christian Brother took the board duster which was in his hand [i.e. a heavy piece of wood with a soft cleaning front], and he threw it at me with a lot of force. It hit me on the side of my head close to my eye leaving a red mark and a bruise. My parents asked me how this had happened, and I made up some story about hurting myself in the play ground. I did dare not tell them the truth.

It is sad for me, some 50 years on, that the main memories of my formative schooling are only for the bad things that happened. To be honest, I was not a very bright pupil. My Mother told me that I suffered from 2nd child syndrome. My elder brother was certainly more intelligent than me and enjoyed education. Indeed, as the first born, I do believe that he was treated differently in many ways. Sister Bernadette, the main teacher, certainly had him down as her favourite, whilst I was "less talented" and unlikely to be successful at passing exams. The truth was that she was right. My brother passed his eleven plus examination with flying colours while I failed mine. My Mum though was terrific. She could see that I was struggling at school, and even on their meagre financial resources [my parents were generally poor], she paid for me to have extra tuition in order to pass my eleven plus exams so that I could go to a good secondary school. Unfortunately, it was wasted. I was a very late learner and I found it hard to concentrate on my lessons. My attention span at that time was very poor, and I was forever in trouble for day-dreaming and not paying attention to proceedings in class. It didn't help that my big brother, two and a half years my senior, was by comparison, "The Brain of Britain". Even as a child, whilst I would read the "Beano", he would sit on the toilet for an age reading "The Encyclopaedia Britannica". You get the general idea of it? He was academic whilst I struggled with most of my lessons. To this day I owe my Mum a huge debt of gratitude, especially, as she paid for private tuition to try to help me pass my Eleven Plus examination. Given that just about everybody in those days was poor [at least where we lived], it was a major sacrifice. However, it was all to no avail, as I failed, and so when I was eleven I was due to go to the Secondary Modern School.

School days were not my favourite time, but as with many Catholic families, school and social life were very much inter-twined. In the fifties, people generally lived, worked, played and socialised within the same town and the same community. Most of our life at that time revolved around the church and school. Dad was a member of the SVP [Saint Vincent de Paul]. He would visit poorer people in our community and help them in whatever way they could. Dad was a very good and kindly man, but goodness knows where he found the time to help others. He worked six and a half days a week as a fitter, at the local aircraft factory, A. V. Roe and Son, better known simply as AVRO, one of the most famous of all British aircraft manufacturers, best known for the iconic AVRO Lancaster bomber. Dad was very proud of this, doing his "bit for the war", as well as being part of the Home Guard. He was too old to fight during the war, and he saw this as doing his part for his country. He worked over-time most evenings, and then he would come home and do jobs like mending our shoes before going to bed. Dad never had enough time, and was always on the last minute and rushing to get to places. I could never understand it, but he would always eat his cornflakes at 11pm at night, because he said that he would not have time to eat his breakfast in the morning! Strange logic, but Dad had many of these eccentricities. He was somewhat hard of hearing and always asking us to repeat ourselves [rather as I do now!], and when we said something that he could not hear, he would put his spectacles on and say "That's better"! I can hear you now! As I say, it was a strange logic, but that's what made my Dad so loveable.

Mum too was very much part of the local community, always involved in Church Socials, and again, like Dad, was part of a Church organisation that helped poorer people in the community. With hindsight, and by today's standards, our family at that time would be part of today's poor. Dad's wage was meagre, and Mum supplemented this with a range of part-time jobs over the years from school dinner lady to evening factory worker, in order to look after her four children. At the time we were no different from all the other families on the estate. We all eked out a living by helping each other and borrowing, when necessary. This was usually by Thursday of each week. Dad's wages and Mum's house-keeping allowance normally stretched until about Wednesday each week – just! It was a regular occurrence for Mum to ask me or one of the other children to go across to Nora Moore, a neighbour, to borrow some milk, bread, butter, jam or whatever item we were without. It was reciprocated regularly, and when the neighbours were short, they would also borrow from us. Of course, Mum always repaid what had been borrowed. Bread and jam for tea [after school] was a normal meal, and sometimes we had butter on it too. Well, not real butter of course, that was for Sundays and special days, but our real treat was bread and "dripping", or even better, toast and "dripping". OK, so it wasn't the healthiest of options but it tasted really good, especially when we were hungry.

With four hungry mouths to feed, Mum had to work hard in order to supplement the income, but it was to have a negative affect on her health. She suffered from chronic chest problems in her younger years, probably due to the damp climate in the area, and the regular smog from the hundreds of factory chimneys dotted around the horizon. In the mid fifties, a scene from Middleton was just like a scene from many of L.S. Lowry's paintings. The scene was full of factory chimneys and people scurrying to and from work. Mum had really bad chest problems as a result, not helped by smoking 20 or 40 "Players Medium" un-tipped cigarettes a week. The sad part was that most people smoked and most children were "passive smokers" and many are suffering respiratory problems today as a result of the smoking and the un-healthy environment at the time. Of course, Mum, just like all her peers was not to blame. She truly believed that smoking was good for her. It helped the nerves and relieved stress. This was the advertising message pumped out to fifties consumers.

The early 1950's were not a great period for healthy living. We had a basic but generally poor diet compared to now. Children had all sorts of diseases that do not largely exist in the 21st century such as ringworm, scurvy, impetigo and all sorts of nasty but not life threatening illnesses, usually caused by poor health conditions and diet. As stated previously, the air and atmosphere in Middleton at the time were particularly poor, so much so that my Mother was warned that if she did not move from Middleton, then she would develop serious respiratory conditions. She needed to move to a location with a cleaner atmosphere. The town of Middleton and its surrounding areas were typical of many Northern Towns in that it had a plethora of high chimneys from factories belching out black smoke into the atmosphere and into people's lungs. Little wonder then that despite actually moving home some years later, to Marple in the Cheshire countryside, the damage had been done and Mum and most of our family have suffered from significant respiratory diseases in later life. Even as a young boy, my elder Brother suffered from Asthma quite badly and for a young nine year old lad, his health was quite fragile. At this time he had been very unwell, badly affected by the damp and smoke filled atmospheres all around us. In those days, it was common for people who had needed operations or been ill to go to what they then called Convalescent Homes. These were establishments, which were usually charitable organisations that cared for people who had come out of hospital after operations. Recovery times then were much longer than nowadays, and a two week stay in a hospital would often require a recovery period of many weeks. Such a place was Freshfields Convalescent Home, set in the small Lancashire town of Formby, and as the name indicated, it was in the middle of fields and countryside. It was therefore a much more peaceful and healthy location for rest and recuperation after illness. Places such as this were not available as part of the newly formed National Health Service. It was organised by what was known as "The Hospital Saturday Fund". This organisation was some type of poorer person's private health scheme. Mum and Dad contributed a small amount each week [sixpence, I think], that's two and a half new pence to you! However, as a result of the contribution paid and the help of the Church, Mum obtained a place for my Brother. His Asthma and general health were very poor and it was thought that he would benefit from the fresh air and open fields. Quite why I went along too, I was never quite sure. I do not remember being ill at the time, but it was thought that it would be good for us both to go to Freshfields for a few weeks to improve our general health and wellbeing.

We took the steam train from Middleton to Manchester and then onto Formby Station where we were met and taken to Freshfields Convalescent Home. It was formerly a Monastery, but then the home was run by the nuns of the Poor Servants of the Mother of God. I was sent there for about three weeks during the summer of 1955. Supposedly, it was to help my brother to regain his health and I went along with him as I had generally been unwell too, after a bout of measles and a rash of cold sores on my face. From the outside, Freshfields looked like a beautiful building in a very pleasant country area, with lovely greenery, and close by were sand dunes and the sandy beach at Formby. All in all it was a beautiful area and the home had the look of an old fashioned country mansion. However, once inside Freshfields, it was entirely a different story. There were between fifty and sixty ill or convalescent children, aged from between three and thirteen years of age. My first impression on entering the home was the smell of stale baked beans and stewed cabbage which permeated the place. At least it smelt that way. The interior walls were a dull and dingy grey, the dormitories had worn metal beds and metal sided cabinets, and the floor was covered with hard linoleum, which was the standard floor covering of the day. Harsh fluorescent lights glared from the ceiling off the stark tiles, and even the regular daily disinfectant could not disguise the sharp aroma of urine and faeces. Like all institutions of its day, life was regulated and regimented, and very, very strict. Here the dangers of too much sympathy and spoiling were clearly pointed out to both children and relatives. It was considered that the child would benefit from not having anxious parents or friends close by. The nuns who ran the home believed strongly that the new patients needed a calm, disciplined and unemotional atmosphere. It did not take long to adjust to this new regime, a day or two at most, so the visiting of sick children was not permitted. Any parcels sent from home were confiscated, stored in the "forbidden" cupboard and eked out slowly by the nuns. Any children, who cried or were badly behaved in any way, would not receive the goodies in the parcel.

Many of the children had their hair cut very short just after arrival in order to prevent the spread of head-lice. The re-assuring night-lights that children had at home were not allowed and the bedside call bells would be removed if they were used by the children too often. The medical care given by the nuns was good, but tea and sympathy were always in very short supply.

My lasting memory of Freshfields is of a very stern nun coming to my bedside at six am every morning [I was only seven years old!] and telling me to get up quickly and get dressed and then hurry along to the chapel to serve the priest at Mass. This happened every day that I was there. The nuns were so strict and although I do believe that they meant well, my stay there reminded me of the images I have since seen, of the old orphanages in Victorian days. I imagined myself as a latter day Oliver Twist, being browbeaten by the Beadle, and then one day, to my relief, it was all over! My Mother was at the home, collected me and my brother, and took us to the train station. I was on my way back to my loving family with my brother. The experience of my stay at Freshfields is one of the worst memories of my young life and it has stayed with me all these years. I have returned to Formby since then to see the building, as I pass that way quite frequently. Of course the building has long since gone and it has now been replaced by new apartments that now occupy the grounds it stood upon. However, even now I get the shivers every time I drive past Freshfields and recall that unpleasant period of my young life.

At this time in Catholic communities, the biggest influence on life was the Parish Priest. He was the Patriarch, and when he spoke, people would listen. He was generally revered and even feared by most of his parishioners, and his influence stretched way beyond the boundaries of his Church and into many aspects of social and personal life. In the early fifties there was a huge influx of Irish Priests coming to live and practice on the English Mainland. There must have been a massive calling of young priests in Ireland, for Ireland itself seemed well catered for in that department, so perhaps there was an overspill of Priests coming to England. For whatever reason, our parish in Langley had four Priests, Fathers Murphy, Walsh, O'Connor and Father O'Driscoll. When you add to this the number of active Irish nuns in the parish, [Sisters Barbara and Bernadette], to name but two, it was easy to see the strict Irish Catholic influence in the parish. Of course, in Ireland, the Catholic Priest took on the mantle of God [almost literally!]. He was the heart and soul of the parish and community, and the Leader in so many aspects of religious and social life.

Most of the good Catholic families were proud to have sons serving the Church as Altar Boys. The same did not apply to the girls in the fifties. Both my elder brother and I were involved in doing the Altar service from an early age of eight years old. We would frequently assist in all the Church services of Mass, Sunday Benediction and various other services such as The Stations of the Cross. We were only kids, but we had to be up early to serve at Mass and do our duty. Of course, kids are kids, and I remember getting rattled across the ear by Father Murphy on more than one occasion for talking in the sacristy or not being as attentive as I should have been. I was never ever hit by my own Father, who was a gentle man, but I had many a clout by the Parish Priest. Even then it did not seem right to me, but times were different then and different standards applied to most aspects of life.

One of the highlights of the Catholic calendar was the Whit Sunday walks. This was when all the Churches, Catholic and other denominations would parade through the parish and the town to demonstrate and show pride in their religion. The Catholics walked on Whit Sunday and the Church of England walked on a different Sunday a week or so later. This was a magnificent event. The entire parish would assemble at Church and we would be bussed into Manchester to parade around the streets and show our belief and faith in our church. All the children would wear brand new clothes, even the poorest, and everybody was in their Sunday marching best. There was a tradition for all the catholic children to put on their "best" new clothes and people would give them money. I was never quite sure why, but it really helped the pocket money, and like all the other kids I would go around to all the neighbours and family so show off my marching clothes, and I would come away with lots of money in the new pockets. When we arrived in Manchester, each parish would have a massive parade banner and would be fronted by a pipe band with a brass band at the rear. In the centre was the heart of the parish, i.e. the Girl Guides and Scouts [all bedecked in their uniforms, the Mothers society, the S.V.P society, the teachers, and all groups of people in any way associated with the parish, all carrying banners of their group, and of the parish. It was almost a competition to see who could be the best. Each church parish would try to put on a better show with more participants than the next parish and everyone was bursting with pride to be a part of their procession and community.

At the head of our Parish Procession, [St.Mary's and St.Columba's of Langley,] strode the four priests, all kitted out in their finest Robes for the occasion. Not only was this a show of strength and faith for our own parish church, it was showing to the world the strength and belief of the Catholics for all to see. Father Murphy, ably accompanied by his three Curates, led the procession and behind them was a huge Pipe Band blasting out a Catholic Marching Hymn called "Faith of Our Fathers". This was the Catholic equivalent of "Land of Hope and Glory". There were thousands of people blasting out this hymn at the top of their voices with belligerent pride. Each parish was trying to out-do each other, and the Catholics were trying to show to the world that they truly believed that this was the one true religion. This was at a time when Christian religions did not respect each other and bigotry abounded. Today's branches of Christianity try to get along and respect each other's differing versions of the Christian belief, but at that time opinions were hardened and other beliefs were not easily tolerated. This was brought into sharp focus by the antics of Christians in Northern Ireland in the 1970's when Catholics and Protestants were marching through Belfast as if it were war. It was never this bad in 1950's Manchester, but neither was it that far away. Even the Catholic marching hymn "Faith of our Fathers", although sung with Gusto and Pride, was indeed provocative, as it referred to the Catholic Martyrs of the Cromwell days and how they were put to death for their belief in Catholicism. As we marched through the streets of Manchester singing this hymn at the top of our voices, and deeply proud of it, most of the young people were not aware of the words they were singing and of the relevance of it all. Nowadays, it would be strictly un-P.C. to sing such hymns as they would be deeply hurtful to the Church of England and other protestant religions and they have been completely discarded from Catholic hymn sheets. One of the main features of all Christian Religions was the way that they would propagate their faith and develop the next generation of clergy. The religion was deep rooted in families and communities and the clergy were highly revered and respected. As such, it was seen as an absolute privilege to have a son in the family who would become a priest. Being a priest was not seen as a job or a profession. Priests and religious orders such as Nuns and Brothers were "called" by God. They did not choose to be a religious person, they were chosen from on high. Of course, people could reject such a calling, but it was not everyone that was chosen, and it was indeed a privilege to be asked to be a Catholic Priest. Already, when I was aged ten my elder brother had already decided to become a priest. Sister Bernadette had always said that he was destined for this office and that he was "special". He was to go to St. Bede's College in Manchester as a border to train to be a priest. He was to go to the junior seminary where he would be initially educated to the correct level before then going to a major seminary to start the long training that would result in him becoming a priest in a parish such as the one we were brought up in.

Quite how I was to follow a similar path, I am not very sure, and time has dimmed the recollection. My elder brother was always my major role model, although we were always very different types of person. I did not have the same intelligence at that time. I was indeed a slow learner and it was only in my late teens that I started to fulfil my potential. The nuns told my parents that I was lazy minded, although I do believe that I was affected by what they now call "2nd child syndrome". The first-born was somehow special and I just somehow got along without ever setting the world alight. So perhaps it came as a surprise to all when I followed in my brother's footsteps. Quite whose idea this was is difficult to say. I had influences coming from all directions of my life. Somehow I very much doubt that it was my decision, at the grand old age of 10 years, to become a Missionary Monk, destined to go to Africa and bring religion to the poor people. In many ways, I must have been a product of my up-bringing. Was it the influence of my parents, the Priests, the Nuns or my brother? We will now never know for sure, but the fact is that I went to an exhibition [yester-years version of the N.E.C], where all the different sectors of religious orders of Catholicism were recruiting for young boys to train as priests and monks. Although I loved my family, school and the nuns and priests that had such an influence on my life, I do not remember having a burning desire at that age to join their ranks. However, I do remember going to this religious exhibition where I was to meet and listen to many types of religious orders. The one that I became attracted to was the Redemptorists, a religious order of Monks who also became Priests and then went to the countries like Africa to preach to and convert the people to Catholicism. Of all the many and various types of Religious Orders and Priests, there was something special about the Redemptorists that stood out from the others. They offered this pioneering lifestyle, half contemplative and half missionary. It was a mix that has an appeal and an excitement even at that very young age and I decided that it was the one for me to join. Quite how I was able to make a decision, at the age of ten, to move away from home to boarding school, with a view to such a drastic life-style change, is still beyond me. It was a momentous decision to leave my parents, brothers and sister, relatives and all my friends to start a new life a hundred miles away, where I would be away from home for most of every year, and quite possibly for the rest of my life. I think I could quite easily have been just as influenced to become a train driver or a footballer at that age. It seemed that I was being swept along on a huge tidal wave and I could not get off. The momentum was carrying me along at a mind-boggling speed. It was as if I was on a train that was hurtling along at 100 miles an hour and I could not get off even if I wanted to. It was a non stop express train to somewhere, but I was not to know when or where it would stop on this journey of a life-time. Of course, my Brother had already taken the big step to becoming a priest. He was two and a half years my senior, and he must have had an influence on me even if it was just in my sub-conscious mind. This was strange in many ways, because although he was my elder brother and a role model, I would often try to do the opposite to him, just to be awkward, or possibly to rebel and build my own independence. While he read books, I would read comics! While he supported Manchester United, I deliberately chose Manchester City, just to be different. So when it became apparent that I was to follow him down the same path to Priesthood, it was a fair bet that I would choose a slightly different route to reach the same destination. Somehow the route I chose seemed more exciting, scarier, and ever more adventurous that the route chosen by my brother to become a Priest in an English Parish. At some stage, at the religious exhibition, somebody had asked me if I wanted to join the order, and I must have said yes. Of course I knew it was a privilege to have a priest in the family, let alone two. Perhaps I felt that I would be letting my parents down if I did not "accept the calling"! All sorts of emotions must have been going on in my young and un-decided mind, but how can a ten year old make such a momentous decision? Yet somehow, somewhere along the line, I realised that I had said "Yes" and before I knew it, I was on a long and winding road that was to take me "Nearly all the way" to the summit. I had failed my Eleven Plus examination, and now it didn't really matter. I was on the road to a life that was to change me for ever and take me on a momentous journey through life which would have many highs and lows, twists and turns, but none the less, a life that I will never regret and will hold dear to me for the rest of my days.

The last few weeks and days at home were unusual. Whilst I knew that I had taken a big decision, I did not fully realise the full significance of it. After all, I was just an eleven year old boy. People would ask me if I was excited about going away to Erdington Abbey, the home of the Redemptorists in Birmingham, and my new home to be, for at least six years. Of course, I told everybody that asked, that I was excited and happy to be moving away from home and family, and yet, inside of me I was scared and nervous. I had fallen in love with an idea, but now that the time had come to go, I was having second thoughts. However, the decision had been made, and family, friends and teachers were all excited on my behalf and I could not now change my mind even if I wanted to. That night, I went to bed, knowing that the next day I would be leaving home. As I lay there, wide awake until the early hours of the morning, I wondered just what it was that I had done. As much as I would argue and fight with my brothers and sister, as all young children do, I could not imagine leaving them for good to only see them at school holiday times. I did not want to leave the young life that I had at home and at school. I would miss all my school friends so much. But more than anything, I would miss seeing my Mum and Dad every day. I had always been very close to them both, and was especially close to my Mum and I wondered what she thought of me going away from home at such an early age. Of course my elder Brother had done the same just two years earlier, but he would be able to come home more often than I would.

I did not sleep that night, as I imagined the change to my life that lay ahead of me. I would be leaving my home, my own bed, school, friends and everything I knew, in order to follow a dream, but would that dream turn into a nightmare? I was about to find out very soon.

Three

Erdington Abbey

The big day arrived! It was the 1st. week of September 1960. I had reached the total of eleven years old, and my 12th birthday in 16 days would be spent away from home.

Out in the big wide world, a new decade was just nine months old and with the promise of great changes ahead. The sixties were to be a bright new era. Everything was about to change. Harold Wilson had promised a new beginning for all. People were buying cars and houses, and were becoming wealthier! The Beatles were about to blast their way into everyone's lives and skirts were about to become minis! Society was about to change drastically, and for me, life was changing too. And how!

On 1st September 1960, I boarded the train at Manchester Victoria Rail Station. My Dad loaded two very large and battered old suitcases into a carriage [we didn't have a car]. I pretended to be very brave as I waved from the train window to the very end of the platform when Mum and Dad were out of sight. Inside I was very nervous. Freshfields apart, I had never left my parents other than to stay a few days with my Aunt Nellie, and I was never going to live at home again [except for holidays], if the grand plan went accordingly. Although it was only a hundred miles away, the journey seemed as if it was never going to end. It was a steam engine train and the carriage was a self contained six seated compartment. Although the train stopped several times at various stations along the way, I sat in this carriage on my own for the entire journey. After what seemed to be an eternity, the train steamed into another station and I finally read the station sign "Erdington". I pulled the two huge suitcases from the overhead compartment, almost knocking myself out in the process, and finally dragged them onto the platform. This was quite an achievement for a 12 year old boy, for although I was quite tall for my age, I was quite skinny and not very strong. I stood there, nervously looking around the platform for a sign of recognition from someone. Eventually, an old lady approached me and in a strong Irish accent said to me: *"You must be Stephen!"*

The lady was Mary O'Flaherty, and she introduced herself to me as the Matron at Erdington Abbey Juvenate. She was to be many things to me over the following six years, Mother substitute, and Nurse to name but two, but whereas my Mother was a loving figure, Matron was a fierce and fiery Irish lady and she cut a figure of someone to be feared and obeyed, in the manner of many institutions of that time. We walked all of 300 yards from the railway station, suitcases being dragged behind me, before entering the foreboding gates to Erdington Abbey which was to be my home for the next six years. The Abbey was an old traditional building comprising a Church with a very tall steeple and an Abbey building which housed the Redemptorist Monks, Priests and Brothers. It was such a commanding presence in the town. Erdington Abbey Church was built in 1848 and is an example of the Gothic Revival Architecture. The church was built by Charles Hansom, who built the steeple of the church 117 ft [36m] high, which is also the length of the building. In 1877 the Benedictine Monks took up residence and in 1880 the first wing of the Monastery was finally completed with The Redemptorist Order taking up residence from the Benedictines in 1922.

My introduction to boarding school life was to come as quite a shock to the system, as this was no ordinary boarding school. Even from such an early age of 12 years, the objective was quite clear. The training and education were all geared up to one goal. It was to be a long and demanding process, but the target was to become a Redemptorist Monk and Priest at some stage in the future, probably by the age of 25 or 26 years. It was to require a good basic education, followed by a specialist training that would require a huge determination and dedication. After all, from aged twelve years to twenty six, meant fourteen years of education in front of me, and I was no academic!, so it was not going to be an easy path to follow; It would require sheer hard work and persistence

The Juvenate at Erdington Abbey was set up to educate the boys, [girls were persona non-grate]. In 1960 at my introduction, there were six forms, aged twelve to eighteen years, with a maximum of fifty boys at any one time. The numbers of boys were dictated by the number of vocations that the Religious Order could recruit, so class sizes at Erdington ranged from twelve in the first year to about six or so at the higher age group, as there were the inevitable fall-outs, with boys leaving. It has always been the strong belief of the Catholic Church that vocations to the Monastic orders and the Priesthood were a calling from God. In simple terms, we were called to the vocation and chosen by God, rather than us choosing this position for ourselves. For a young boy, it was quite something to take to heart, and especially at that early age, it felt like something of a responsibility, even a burden to carry.

The change in lifestyle was very sudden and stark. Although I had "chosen" this path myself, this life-style, it was hugely different from the normal family life of its time. Just being away from my parents, brothers and sister, [I had two brothers and one sister], was quite traumatic and I was to find it hard to come to terms with.

I was allocated my bed in a dormitory of ten boys. The beds were adequate, if not comfortable and alongside it was a bedside cabinet for my personal belongings. At the end of the dormitory were a row of cupboards [wardrobe would be too complimentary!], and all my clothes for that term were to be kept there. Perhaps it was a sign of the times, but a shirt had to last for one week, underpants were two for a week and socks were just three pairs a week. Pyjamas had to last for a full week. Clean laundry was given out weekly, so we were not the sweetest smelling of boys, but that's how it was in the early 1960's. I was so very nervous on the first night at the Juvenate. Why? Well I had a shocking secret! Right up until my first day at boarding school, I had regularly wet the bed whilst living at home. This occurrence was not every night, but it was quite regular, and at the age of eleven years, I should have been past that stage of my boyhood. I don't know why I wet the bed, and why I had this problem. I imagine a psychologist would have a field day in deciphering the possible causes. To be frank, I was not at all bothered as to the cause of bed-wetting. I was just hoping and praying that I would not wet my bed on my first night away from home. I would be a laughing stock with the other boys, and what would the Matron think? I would be mortified! My first night arrived and I deliberately did not have a drink much after lunch time. Maybe that would help? I went to bed that night, petrified that I would make a fool of myself and be shamed in front of the others. After a nervous night I fell asleep and woke at about 5.30am. Nervously I felt around the bed and with a huge feeling of relief, not to say surprise, the whole of the bed was dry. The next night was the same, and the next one, and the one after that, and miraculously, I never wet the bed again. Make of that whatever you can, but I have no idea how or why things changed. All of a sudden, I had grown up overnight, at least in that situation.

The daily routine for weekdays was extremely regimented. It started at 6am with a very rude awakening. At what seemed like the middle of the night, the Juvenate Director would burst into the Dormitory. There was no gentle awakening and from the bottom end of the dormitory he shouted something in Latin that sounded like "Gaudete"! [This was the Latin for "Rejoice"] a good morning greeting, but it did not feel like it! At that, he burst down the dormitory throwing the bed-clothes off those boys that had not immediately leapt from bed. We had to reply likewise in Latin and immediately fell to our knees by the side of the bed and recite "Ave Maria" It was a robotic mumbled response and usually spoken through tired mouths and minds. Within minutes it was off to the bathroom for a quick wash and dress into the school uniform and by 6.30am, we all had to congregate in the chapel for morning meditation. This was to consist of kneeling in the chapel for thirty minutes and contemplate life. It was meant to be a time for personal prayer with God and to consider the meaning of life and beyond. In the early days, I must confess that contemplation and meditation were synonymous with sleeping. I mean, how does a twelve year old boy understand the meaning of meditation? As the years progressed I did get rather better at it, but at first it seemed like a form of torture and something that had to be endured. I would kneel in the pew, elbows cupping my head and try hard to contemplate the meaning of God, of life or anything holy. Of course, the mind often drifted away and I was just as likely to be contemplating what we were going to have for breakfast.

After meditation, we had Mass every morning at 7am followed by communion. In keeping with the times, Mass was always conducted in Latin. Initially, it was just like reciting something in a foreign language, but of course we had been brought up with the Latin Mass, and although none of the younger boys really knew what they were saying, they were aware that it was prayer and that would suffice. Latin was of course to be one of the main lessons in our curriculum so in time we did have an understanding of what we were saying everyday. Although the Mass was the bedrock of the Catholic Religion, I could not help the feeling that it was trotted out in "parrot fashion" every morning into something of a ritual. It felt like something that had to be done, but there was no real feeling to it. Mass would last from between twenty minutes and half an hour on a weekday, and we would take it in turns to be Altar Boys and assist the Priest at Mass. Normally this would be in the chapel within the Juvenate, but as there were around a dozen or so priests in Erdington Abbey, each priest would celebrate Mass every day in a personal type of ritual. At the centre of the Abbey there was the main Church Altar where services were carried out for the local congregation, but there were also several other altars around the Church perimeter and a priest and an Altar Boy would go and "celebrate" Mass [in Latin], just the two of them, each morning. I used to like serving Mass in the main Abbey; it made a change from the normal service each day in the Juvenate Chapel. By this time, I had learned "parrot fashion" of course, the entire liturgy of the Mass in Latin and I could recite the entire Mass in Latin, both for the priest's part and my own responses.

Come 7.30am each weekdays, Mass was completed and it was off to the refectory for breakfast. This consisted of Cereal [Cornflakes or Puffed Wheat], followed by a cooked breakfast, of a kind. As young and energetic boys, we needed a good breakfast to see us through the day, but a healthy breakfast it was not! For the next six years, Monday to Saturday, I was to have fried bread and beans as my breakfast, every day! The fried white bread was absolutely wet and soggy and saturated in grease. It was then loaded with a large dollop of baked beans. Strangely, most of us loved it. It was stodgy, and it filled us up, and of course there is something quite comforting about eating fat! Of course, I did not know it at the time, but six years of eating fried bread and beans every day had an effect on my constitution, and by the age of twenty one, I would have to have an operation for a duodenal ulcer in my stomach. I could never have been sure that it was caused by the fried bread and beans, but I think that it was the prime culprit. It was not helped by the type of barter arrangement that I had going with another boy called Conrad Potts, who was in my year. He was not a lover of Fried Bread and Beans, so after I had eaten mine, he would give me his and I would devour that too. After all, I was as skinny as a rake at that time and I had boundless energy. I needed all the protein I could get. In return for his breakfast, I would give him my pudding every day at lunch-time. It wasn't that I didn't like the puddings; it was just that I preferred the fried bread and beans!

After breakfast finished at 8am, it was time to make own beds and we were all allocated a job to do around the Juvenate. It was a type of housework before breakfast. Jobs would change from time to time, but basically, the fifty or so boys at the Juvenate would then spend half an hour doing the housework before lessons commenced. My first job was cleaning one of the longest corridors I had ever seen! I would have to sweep a one hundred feet long corridor clean, of all the previous day's dirt, and then armed with a mop and bucket I would mop the corridor from top to bottom, making sure it was dry enough to walk safely upon. Matron would patrol the entire building like some sort of "work warden", making sure that the jobs were done efficiently, and until she had signed off your job to her satisfaction, you could not continue with your next part of the day. Jobs were over and 8.30am came around. This usually meant about thirty minutes of free time, and most of us would take the opportunity to have a walk around the grounds before lessons began. We would perhaps kick a football around, or just have a natter with our friends before going into the first lesson that day.

Nine O'clock arrived and the school bell sounded. My first class consisted of eleven other boys, just like myself, from all parts of the country, and with similar life ambitions. The main objective was that in years to come, we would all become Monks and Priests of the Redemptory Order. Of course, at this stage we were just a group of scallywags, a mere group of boys in their first day at a new school. Not that this was any type of ordinary Secondary Modern or Grammar School. You only had to glance at the school syllabus to see that there was a different agenda, even though at the age of twelve, the objective was to have a normal type of education. High on the syllabus were such lofty subjects as Latin, Greek, French, Spanish, English Literature, and Art to name but six. This was not a range of subjects that was going to educate me for a job in industry when I was of working age, but it was an ideal syllabus for the life-style I was about to start upon.

During the school day, we would have a succession of teachers; all of them were Redemptorist Priests or Brothers. Each would ply his subject for forty five minutes to an hour, after which the bell the ring, and the next teacher would enter the classroom and it was then onto the next subject.

Lunchtime was a pretty formal affair in the refectory. The meal was plain but fairly wholesome, the usual meat and two vegetables. This was always followed by a good old stodgy pudding, chocolate cake and custard, rice or sago pudding with jam or something similar. Of course, I was always hungry at lunch times because I had this ongoing deal, whereby I had already mortgaged my daily pudding to Conrad Potts, for my daily double fix of fried bread and beans at breakfast time, but it was a pretty fair deal.

Strangely, in the refectory was a pulpit, and at the start of the meal, the food was eaten in silence, except for one boy who would sit in the pulpit and read to the rest of the boys during our meal. At lunch times, this usually consisted of a book, usually a biography or some similar topic, but at evening meal times, again mainly eaten in silence, there would be a religious theme, usually the life story of a saint, or a similarly uplifting topic. Towards the end of lunch, the reading would finish and we would talk as much as we wanted for the rest of the meal, about everyday boyish things. Believe it or not, we were a very normal group of kids but in a very unusual and abnormal setting, but we were just the same as other young lads.

After lunch, there was a recreation period until 2pm. Most of us were football mad we would go down to the soccer pitch. It was more of a ploughed field really, and we would kick a ball around for half an hour or so.

Then it was back to lessons again until 4.30pm. On the face of it, it was a fairly normal school day, but unlike kids on the outside, we had to go back into classroom later, for two hours of gruelling homework. After we took our afternoon tea, usually bread and jam, we would have half an hours break to get some fresh air or do something different, and then at 5.30pm it was back to the classrooms for home-work. Every lesson during the day finished with the teacher handing out a dollop of homework, so we were kept fully busy every weekday evening, and this would have to be completed and handed in for marking at the next lesson.

It seemed like a long day, every day, and then at 7.30 pm we had finished the formal day's activities and we had an hour and a half to ourselves for recreation. It was just about the only time of day when we could do almost whatever we wanted, as long as we remained in the confines of the building and the grounds. Outside, we did have quite a lot of land on which to play, including a football pitch, small woods, a pig sty and a farm area. There was also a large formal garden but that was mainly frequented by the Monks and Priests and we generally kept out of their way. If the weather was bad or it was dark or if we just wanted to stay indoors, we had our own "common room" where we would relax in a variety of ways, snooker, playing records or just generally chatting.

Come 9 pm and that was it! The end of the day had arrived. The school bell would sound, and as soon as it did, no matter what we were doing, we would stop immediately and make our way up to the dormitories. Then it was off to the wash-rooms, clean teeth, get the mud of the day off, and get in to the jim-jams and then go straight into bed by 9.15 pm. As a twelve year old boy, I did not mind this too much as I was usually worn out by this time and morning would come around again, all too soon. But by the end of my time at Erdington, by which time I was almost 18 years old, I was not too pleased to have to be in bed by 9.15 every evening. The Juvenate Director would come around to the dormitories at 9.15 pm, and after a short set of bedtime prayers, kneeling by the side of our bed, it was straight into the bed and the lights went out. This meant no talking at all until the next morning. Each dormitory had a "monitor", usually from the 6th form, and he would be in charge during the night until the following morning. He would enforce the "no talking" and "no pranks" curfew.

So that was the typical type of weekday at the Juvenate. Weekends were generally different and we had much more recreation and freedom to do other things, like playing football, going for walks, listening to records and watching T.V. Of course, this was the start of the "swinging 60's and although we were hardly typical of that young and vibrant generation, we were certainly children of our time, and were just as involved in many things that kids in normal schools did. Of course, the new Pop Culture was in full swing. We developed our own Pop club where we all put money in each week and paid into a record club. The exact amount escapes me, but it was probably about six old pence, two and a half pence in today's money, but clubbed together, we managed to buy at least one new record every week. Of course, the top acts at the time were none other than The Beatles, Rolling Stones, Cliff Richard and groups like the Kinks. Although, like the others, I was a big fan of these, when my turn came around I chose a record called "Let's Get Together" by Hayley Mills! Now who would have thought that Hayley Mills would have had a top 20 hit, but she did. I got a lot of stick for choosing that record because a lot of my mates wanted to go for the new Rolling Stones record, which had just gone to the top of the charts about the same time. However, I had recently been to the cinema to watch Hayley Mills in a new film called "The Parent Trap" and I fell in love with her, [although she never knew it], and so I bought the record and played it until the track had almost been worn smooth.

We had two recreation rooms at The Juvenate, one for the eleven to fifteen year olds and the other for the sixteen years plus. Each had a TV set, a record player, a full size snooker table and a selection of books and suitable reading material. We would spend many an hour in these, usually during evening recreation period and at weekends. We would chat, play records, discuss music, and we would even discuss "Girls" even though young females would never be allowed to enter the building at all. We were still normal boys, and despite the objective of eventually leading a future celibate life, girls at that time were very much on our agenda, even if it was just a private topic, it was one which we all chatted about.

Television in the early 1960's was pretty poor and there was not much of it. It only started about mid afternoon and finished about eleven at night. Even so, we were not allowed to watch much television at all. Occasionally, we were allowed to watch the Telly, but the programmes were chosen by the Priests. On one occasion, we all wanted to watch the famous Cassius Clay, AKA Mohammed Ali, fighting Sonny Liston for the World heavyweight Boxing title. This was a massive fight at the time. The programme was on TV at ten O'clock at night. Of course, it was bedtime and lights out for us at 9.15 pm, so it was not possible. But some of the lads decided that despite the rules, we were going to watch it anyway. So, slowly, after lights out and we were left to go to sleep, some of the lads decided that we really wanted to watch the fight. The dormitory slowly emptied, even the "Monitor" and we filed downstairs to the common room to watch the fight. Surely we would not be found out? But yes, just as the fight was reaching its climax, the dark was shattered by a bright light from a torch, and in the doorway stood the dark and threatening figure of Father Minson. He was incandescent with rage! The room light went on so that he could see all the perpetrators who had dared to leave their beds. One by one we filed past him and back to bed, so that he could get a good look at who had defied him. Yes, I was there too, although I was no rebel, I was no saint. When morning came, Father Minson got up and spoke at breakfast, and he read out by name those who had gone to watch TV and for each, there was a punishment of early bed for three nights at 8pm instead of 9.15pm, and detention for three nights for two hours each night. I felt as if I had committed the crime of the century, and that we had been punished as such. Perhaps this was our training for life under a vow of obedience.

To make matters worse, the detention for breaking the bedtime curfew was at the weekend, when we would normally play football or enjoy ourselves. The punishment was hardly stimulating. We had to write out one hundred lines saying: *"I must not be disobedient by watching television after night-time curfew"* It was the most boring of punishments and if that was completed before the two hour detention was up, we had to do an exercise in Latin. Needless to say, I do not remember anybody breaking that curfew again during my time at Erdington.

Father Minson was indeed a very strong disciplinarian and it was not difficult to fall foul of him. He could have his kind and humorous moments, but for each of these he would have many more of his angry ones. As the Juvenate Master, he would effectively take the place of our own fathers while we were at the Juvenate, but to call him Fatherly would be nothing like the truth. He could in no way be called kindly. If indeed he instilled anything into us during the years he was in charge, it would be discipline and good order. In addition, he was also our Latin tutor. Latin was never an easy subject to master and it was also quite alien in many ways, possibly because it was a dead and historic language. I have lost count of the number of times I was forced to write lines in Latin because of not paying attention in class. The line was: *"Oportet operam ad lectio Latina".* In English, the Latin line meant: *"I must pay attention in Latin lessons!"* Father Minson would always be annoying because of his insistence of always speaking to us in Latin even outside of class. If we were ever to ask him permission for anything, his stock reply would be: *"Videbimus".* In English; it means "We will see". He would do this all day and everyday which was really annoying. Anytime you spoke to him about anything, he would answer in Latin and expect you to translate it before he would allow you to do whatever it was that was asked for. He would tell us that by doing this we would be able to speak Latin much more easily, but as Latin had not actually been spoken as a genuine language for several hundred years I did wonder quite what the point of it was.

In fairness, it was still the language of the Catholic Church at the time and every church service was totally in Latin, despite the fact that most members of the congregation had no idea what they were saying or listening to. Thankfully, within the next ten or twenty years, it was all to change and Mass and all the church services would then be celebrated in the English language, at least in our country.

With the benefit of hindsight, I am now glad that I learned Latin. At the time, I would absolutely detest it, but in later years I would come to recognise the benefits of it. It is without doubt the basis of the English Language as well as French, Spanish and several other countries' native tongue. Even nowadays, when I am trying to recognise the meaning of a word either in English or other languages, I still go back to the Latin and recognise it as the base of that particular word or phrase. Thank you to Father Minson!

Four

Mixing with the Parish:

We did not often mix with the local community in Erdington. Occasionally we would go into town to the shops at Weekends or take a walk around the park, or even go to the local library, either get a book or to catch up with the news by reading the national newspapers in the reading room. We did not have newspapers at the Juvenate, so to go out to the library was a real treat.

At The Abbey, we had occasional access to TV, but in those days of the mid-sixties, there were only two channels anyway, and we were only seldom allowed to watch it. Every year we would play the local Erdington Parish football team, the Erdington Colts, which took on the aura of a local Derby. It was usually a feisty affair with local pride at stake, and it was one of the few occasions where we met the locals. Erdington Colts V Abbey St.Edmonds was our big match of the year. Our team name was Abbey St. Edmunds and it was an occasion and a match that we looked forward to. In all the six years I was there, we lost every game that we played against them. The other big moment for mixing outside of the Juvenate, was our annual trip and visit to the Redemptorist Students at Hawkstone Hall. Every year, we would travel the forty or so miles across country from Erdington to Hawkstone Park in Shropshire. This gave us a taste of where we were planning to live in future years. Hawkstone Hall was the senior seminary for Redemptorist students and monks, who were training to become priests and missionaries. So it was an interesting visit every year to see the life-style and to meet the students. The annual visit to Hawkstone was quite an experience for us all and one which we eagerly looked forward to each year. If nothing else, it was a full day out on a coach trip, and it broke up the strict routine of our normal life at Erdington. At the time of each visit, I used to wonder if I would in fact ever get to live there, but it seemed such a long way off in the future. For the time being we concentrated on the bi-annual football match between the Hawkstone Redemptorists and Abbey St.Edmonds. The average age of our team was fifteen to sixteen years old, while the Hawkstone students were around twenty three to thirty. The Juvenate team was generally the more skilful, but the seminary students were so much physically stronger than we were and invariably they would end up winning most of the matches between us.

Back at Erdington, the Church was very much at the centre of the local community and was very well supported by the local people. Religion was still playing a large part in the lives of the locals at that time, and the Church and Community Centre were at the hub of most of the things that happened in the town. At the Juvenate though, we had our own chapel for our own daily services such as Mass and Meditation, and by and large we did not come into regular contact much with the parishioners at Erdington. We were very much isolated in the Juvenate with only occasional visits outside of its walls. There were exceptions of course. We would play football against the local Catholic Church School, which was just around the corner from us. The pupils there viewed us as something of a novelty, and with a degree of suspicion. They generally thought that we were strange and not like other boys, and in many ways they were of course correct. For this reason there was always something of a friction between us, and this would show in a form of physical aggression during the football match.

In the sixties, the Church was generally well attended and there was a thriving Church and Community Centre for the local people at Erdington. It was run as a normal parish, and as well as Holy Mass everyday, there were many other services during the week such as Benediction, The Stations of the Cross and as Altar Boys we would assist at many of the Church Services, where additional solemnity was required. On the lead up to the big Church occasions like Easter and Christmas the Juvenists would be asked to sing in the choir at the parish services.

There we were, bedecked in our flowing red cassocks with white tops. The Juvenate Choir of some thirty angelic looking boys cut quite an impressive sight in the Parish Church. As part of our training we had regular choir lessons in school to learn the words, harmonies and tunes of the hymns, and the various chants at Church services. Individually, our voices may not have been any better than many other boys, but when trained and harmonised, it was not only an impressive sight, but it created an excellent sound too. The choir was a major attraction to the parish. It was also an opportunity to do something outside of the Juvenate itself, but these occasions were not frequent. As with all choirs there were a few boys with really top voices who took the soprano roles, but although I had a reasonable voice, I was still among the body of the choir that sang the chorus lines. Who was to know that many, many years later, I would take on the persona of the one and only Elvis Presley and perform his concerts too.

Even so, I would always volunteer for choir duty as quite regularly it would mean that we would get an opportunity to go outside. Of the fifty or so at the Juvenate, the choir only required between twenty five and thirty of the boys. I would make sure that I was one of the better singers so that I would be selected for the choir and get to go on the "special days" out. There were occasions when we would go the Cathedral in Birmingham for special Church services where the choirs were needed. At least it was an opportunity to see a new place, and we knew that there would be a good meal laid on afterwards. It certainly made a break from the normal routine at Erdington

On one occasion close to Christmas, one of the choir boys suggested an idea to the Choir Master, that it would be good for the parish if we could go out at evenings around Erdington singing Christmas Carols around the town. The Choir Master thought that it was a terrific idea and obtained permission from the Juvenate Director for us to sing carols around the parish between 8pm and 9.30pm. This meant that we avoided the 9.15pm night-time curfew and we did not get to bed until gone 10pm. We did this on four evenings in mid-December. Fortunately, the Choir Master, to the best of our knowledge, never realised that there was an ulterior motive in singing the Christmas Carols to the local parish people. We got to stay up later!

Five

The Confessional

The Catholic Church is well known for being one of the few faiths that believes in the forgiveness of sin, by use of the confessional. Of all the Christian Churches, it is only in the Catholic Church that members confess their sins to a Priest and are then forgiven by God. We had been brought up to believe that, no matter how good we were, or tried to be, that we were all sinners and every week we would need go to the confessional in Church and confess all our wrong-doings to a priest and seek forgiveness.

As a child, this was a very scary part of our life. Sins could be forgiven by God via the priest, but only if indeed you were sorry for committing them. If you wanted to go to heaven when you died, then you must be free of serious sin at that time. If however you were not sorry, then sins could not be forgiven. Certain of the sins were known as "venial" sins, and other more heinous sins were known as "Mortal sins". The massive difference was that venial sins which were less serious, could be forgiven, but that Mortal sins, for serious crimes, could also be forgiven, but only if confessed while you were alive. The teaching of the Church at that time was that if you died without confessing a mortal sin, then when you died, you would go to hell for all of eternity. However, we were not just talking about murders or really serious crimes, but to fail to attend Mass on a Sunday was deemed to be a Mortal Sin. As a child, we accepted this teaching and I am sure that I did not miss Mass on a Sunday, unless I was ill, for very many years. At the young age of twelve and sixteen, this used to terrify me, and often it was a huge relief each week to go to Church at Erdington and confess my sins. But what constitutes a sin to a child? For most of us I image that the sort of sins that would be confessed would be disobedience, bad thoughts, being angry, or similar everyday activities. Even being unkind to someone was deemed as a venial sin and would need to be confessed.

The confessional in a Church was quite a daunting place to be. It is usually a wooded structure with a place for the priest to sit on one side, and a place for the person confessing on the other side. The person confessing his sins would kneel and speak to the priest through a section of blacked out gauze so that they could not be seen and recognised. That would be too embarrassing. Often, the priest would know who was confessing anyway, as the priests and people would know each other and would recognize their voices. However, that was by the by. The Catholic Priest is sworn to secrecy for all matters in the confessional, irrespective of whether the sin is a serious crime, and there have been countless occasions in history where crimes [i.e. sins], have been confessed by guilty people, but the priest would never divulge information gained in his confessional. In the main though, people would confess their sins to the priest, many would do so every week, and the priest would listen, advise them and then give a penance [a small punishment] for the sins, which would then be forgiven by God, through the priest.
At the Juvenate, this took on even more relevance. We were young boys, but we were training to become Monks,

and then Priests. Our standards were perhaps expected to be higher. After all, we were training to become senior members of the Church and we were supposed to be aiming for perfection in our behaviour. This was quite a burden, a mountain of expectation, for a group of young boys. Because our expectations had been set so high, any fault, any sin, was a fall from grace and guilt became an integral part of our life. Certainly it was for me. Every failure had to be examined. Each morning during early morning meditation, we would examine what we had done right, and more importantly, what we had done wrong during that day, and that week. When the time for confessing came, usually on a Friday evening, it was just like unburdening ones-self from all the guilt built up from the sins of that week. It was quite nerve-wracking going into the confessional. I had been waiting in the pews for the previous boys who had made their confession. Sometimes you could hear what was being said if either the boy or the priest spoke too loudly. Of course, you would try not to listen, but it was often difficult not to hear. In some ways, it was re-assuring to hear that other people were no better or no worse than I was, but anyway, I was taking no chances and I would always speak very quietly when I made my confession. It would begin with: *"Bless me Father for I have sinned, it is one week since my last confession"* and I would then go on to tell the priest a list of faults and sins committed since my last confession. The priest would then listen to the confession, give advice, and then give out a penance. This usually consisted of repeating regular prayers, often The Lords Prayer, or Hail Mary a number of times. The norm was for The Lords Prayer twice and then three Hail Mary's. The sins had already been forgiven by the priest in the confessional, but the penance had to be completed afterwards. When you believe as strongly as I believed at that time, it was a huge relief to come out of the confessional and feel that I had a new start, a clean sheet and a huge feeling of relief, that I could try all over again and be a good person, at least for the following week.

Of course, we knew all the priests, some of them were our tutors, but we all had our favourite that we preferred to confess to. One of the favourites for the Juvenate boys was Fr. Charlie McParland. He was nick-named by us as "Three Hail Mary's". We spoke about confessions to each other and we often discussed the different priests and how they were in the confessional. Some were more severe than others, and we knew that they may recognise us from our voices. Some of the boys would try and disguise their voices so as to remain anonymous. I even used to do it myself on occasions by either speaking in a higher or a more gruff voice so as not to be recognised! The great thing about "Charlie McParland" is that no matter what sins you committed, within reason, you would always get three Hail Mary's as the penance. We often joked that if you murdered your Granny, you would still get the same penance of three Hail Mary's. This of course was the lighter side of a serious subject. In truth, I took the matter very seriously. This was our belief, and sins, confession and forgiveness were all part of being a Catholic and a Christian. Although attitudes in the Church were beginning to change in the Sixties, the teaching about sin, heaven and hell were still very traditional and especially in the Religious Orders such as the Redemptorists. The

Catholic teaching was absolutely black and white, with no shades of grey. If you lived a good life and died in a state of grace, then you would go to heaven for all of eternity. But the other side of that equation was that if you led a bad life, and you died in a state of sin, without confessing those sins, and those sins were mortal, then you would indeed go to hell for all of eternity. I remember being taught this at my junior school, when I was between the ages of seven and ten, and it was extremely frightening for any young person. In those days it seemed to be that religion was based on the law of fear, rather than the rule of love. It seemed to me that there was no difference between a mass murderer, who was truly evil, such as many we have known in history, and a person who tries to be good, but maybe missed Mass on a Sunday and then died on the Monday, before getting the chance to confess on the next Friday. According to the Church's Law, that person had committed a mortal sin, and if he died at that point, then he would go to hell for all of eternity. It was not difficult to imagine the affect that this teaching could have on any person, let alone a young and scared child.

It was normal for young Catholic children to start making confessions at the age of around seven. That is about the time when he or she reaches the age of reason and can be held accountable for what they do. At this stage, a child takes Confirmation and afterwards they could make regular Confessions to the priest. You can only imagine the type of sin that a seven year old might confess to the priest, it would hardly be anything to be shocked about, but it enabled them to get into the habit of going to Confession every week and trying to be a good person.

At our age in the Juvenate, between twelve and sixteen, the sins that we committed were almost certainly of the trivial kind, although in our minds these could often be blown up out of all proportion, as worry, guilt and uncertainty would take over. At the Juvenate, we would attend Mass everyday, and sometimes, more than once a day. I remember on one occasion serving at Mass at three separate times during one day. Surely that should have earned me lots of Brownie points. One of the situations that I found it hard to come to terms with in my mind was the following scenario; that if someone had committed what they believed to be a mortal sin, then they were not allowed to go to Holy Communion until the sins had been forgiven. To do so would be another mortal sin, and it would make the matter worse. At the Juvenate, we had a group of boys, all trying to be as good as we reasonably could, but many believed through their guilt and insecurity, that they had committed more serious sins. Because of this, there were many times when during Mass, many of the boys would not take communion because they believed that they may have committed a mortal sin, and that they could not receive communion until they had been forgiven by God. As a Catholic and particularly in the Juvenate life, it was such a relief to be able go to confession and to confess what we believed to be our sins and to know that at least until the next time, everything would be made alright.

Six

The Matron

Mary O'Flaherty was the Juvenate Matron. She was the epitome of everything that a Hospital Matron used to be in the nineteen fifties. She was an older lady, and must have been in her mid seventies at the time. But, instead of retiring and taking life easy, she took on the challenging job of Matron at the Redemptorist Juvenate at Erdington

She was strong, authoritative, domineering and the sort of person that just gets things done. Yes, she could be scary too, although, she did have a kinder side, but she was very slow to show it off, as this could easily be interpreted as a sign of weakness by the teenage boys in her care.

From the first day she met me at the station until many years later, she was all sorts of a person to me. She was a surrogate mother, a nurse, a teacher a disciplinarian, a sometimes friend, but she was always viewed as being on the "other side". She belonged to the establishment, and was one of the priest's assistants who cared for us and controlled us. Of course, ours was an unusual situation. The Matron and the Priests were more than teachers to us. They were taking the place of our parents in many ways. They were bringing us up; they were responsible for our well-being, our health, our education and our overall development. Of course, it was an impossible task. There was just one Matron to act as the female influence to around fifty teenage boys, and to be responsible for our mental, physical and emotional well-being, for around six important years of our young teenage lives. She also had the difficult task of controlling us, making us develop as young men and disciplining us. We were in her care for three terms of each year. As we only went home for a week at Christmas, two weeks at Easter, and then six weeks in the summer, we were under her control for around forty four weeks of the year. I also imagine that this was not a paid position. I believe she did the job for the love of it. It was no small task. As a 63 year old adult, I recently visited the cemetery where she now rests. She eventually lived well into her nineties and is buried in the grounds of the Church at Erdington Abbey. Strangely, although I had not thought of her for quite some time, and it must have been forty years since I actually saw her, I had a strange feeling whilst standing at her grave. It is not a feeling I can explain, except to say that I had a feeling of closeness to her for the six years that I had been under her care. My overwhelming feeling was one of real gratitude for the years of selfless service she had dedicated to us.

It is the small things that I recall about her that leave the lasting memories. She ran a tuck shop at the Juvenate during recreation periods of the evening. She would make the most lovely home made Ginger Beer for three pence a glass, and it was to die for. She had this marvellous ginger plant on her window-ledge and all she did was feed it regularly with sugar, and it went on forever providing us with gallons of this lovely drink. She also made the most wonderful home made fudge. It's a shame that she was not a bit stricter with us about brushing our teeth, because

I lost a lot of my teeth between the age of twelve and sixteen years with plenty of fillings too, but then again, how do you make fifty children brush their teeth twice a day and do the right things, all of the time. It was an impossible task, even for our Matron. There was no doubt that Matron could be seen as an ogre at times, but there were also occasions when her hard and frosty façade would drop and we would see her gentler side. There were of course many times when we would miss our parents and family, particularly when we were ill. On one such occasion I was very much in pain due to sunburn. I made the mistake that many young people make with the sun, by under-estimating its strength, and after playing football in the mid afternoon sun, and without a shirt on, and then getting all hot and sweaty, I lived to regret it. I showered and put my shirt back on and could not stand the shirt on my back. It had blistered and was blood red. Matron sent me immediately to the Juvenate Infirmary. I didn't expect any sympathy at all, because it was my own entire silly fault. But she showed me a side that I had never seen before. She put ice on my back and then very, very gently, she put burn cream all over my back, realising that it was red raw. I was in agony and she took care of me in a way that I was not expecting. She showed a very caring side which she had not often shown before.

More often though, she could be what we would refer to as: "A Battle-Axe" She was a sturdy, well-built woman with a physique and a temper to match. Her red hair tied up in bun and her fast Irish accent belied a wicked Irish temper, and "woe-betides" any of the boys who would get on the wrong side of her. Some of the boys would deliberately try and cajole her and they would then make fun of her, just so that they could see her fly into one of her famous "tempers! I think they just liked to hear her when Matron let-rip at them for not doing what they were told or for playing pranks which they frequently did. While the boys pretended to be afraid of her, most of us actually quite liked her deep down. She was a good woman and very kind and had the thankless task of looking after sixty mischief making boys. I very much doubt that this was a salaried job and I believe that she did it solely for the love of the job and not for any income that she may have been paid for doing it.

After leaving the Juvenate and moving onto Perth and then Hawkstone, I would always contact Matron when I could, often writing to her, particularly at Christmas to see how she was getting along. I had a soft spot for this frosty and occasionally difficult lady, because I knew that deep-down she had a good heart and that she gave up a lot to look after me and the other boys for six years of our lives.

Seven

Junior Education

The Juvenate was all about education and induction into the Monastic Life. Most of us, fifty boys in total, were between eleven and seventeen years old. At the Juvenate, the emphasis was on a good general education. It was not quite the same syllabus as a normal county secondary or grammar school education, but it was as normal as it could be. The education at the Noviciate in Perth was definitely religious, and nothing else, whilst the education at Hawkstone was decidedly scholarly with Philosophy, Psychology and Church History were high on the agendas.

The Juvenate at Erdington attempted to offer a thorough grounding in a classical education. It was quite a syllabus for an eleven year old. It featured highly on Mathematics, English Language, English Literature, Geography, French, Spanish, Art and of course, Latin and Religious studies.

When I considered the fact that I failed my Eleven plus examination, it was something of a daunting task. The truth is that I did not make a great start. Despite being in a small class of only twelve boys, and getting plenty of individual tuition, I was a definite slow starter. For the first three years or so, I was always eleventh or twelfth out of twelve in the class examination results. It didn't auger too well for the future, but things were to get better in years to come as the slow starter began to sprint to the finishing line. There will be more about that in later chapters, but there was one particular example which I will be forever proud of. Alright, I was never very good at Art. We were taught Art by Brother Alphonsus, a 72 year old Religious Brother in The Redemptorists. He was certainly no teacher, and he had no real training in how to teach, but he was a terrific artist and he tried his best, without much luck in my case, in trying to get us to learn the basics of drawing and painting. I did not easily grasp the principles involved in drawing and invariably, term after term, when the exam results for Art were pinned onto the school notice board, the name "NEAREY" was almost always in twelfth place. It was a decent success one year when I was placed in tenth position albeit with a score of 28% out of 100%. However, my day was still to come, and after four years of abysmal art results, my day did in fact arrive. Instead of the usual horizons, trees, or inanimate objects, we were asked to do a "scene." I chose to do a scene from the Nativity. Well it was the Christmas end of term. Now whether I had been struck by brilliance, or perhaps the other class members were having an off day, I never found out, but I knew that I had done a decent drawing. Even so, I still expected to finish bottom, believing that the others would do even better. With some trepidation, I went to look at the notice board and started at the bottom going upwards. Strangely, my name was not there. As I continued up the page the percentages went higher and higher and as I read the top score it said: No.1 NEAREY 79% out of 100%. I was walking on Water! Even my tutor was dumfounded and asked me if someone else had drawn the nativity scene for me. Even he could not believe it. Life at the Juvenate was not all about learning and prayers. After all, we were a group of some fifty healthy boys and most of us were keen on football and other sport. We had a soccer pitch at the Abbey but in truth, it was a bumpy, rough and threadbare pitch; a strange shape, but with goalposts at either end, so it would suffice. We would play football just about every day at lunchtime and sometimes after tea and playing among ourselves was alright, but became a bit tiresome with the same lads everyday. In our third year, when I was fourteen, our principal Fr. Minson agreed that we would form a team and join an outside league with teams from as far a field as ten miles away from Erdington Abbey. It was unusual for us mix much with the outside world, other than an occasional walk into Erdington. When we joined the football league, we were completely out of our depth at first, being hammered regularly by five, six or seven goals and I remember one particularly painful game where we lost by eleven goals to one. Fr. Minson told us we had to toughen up as we were frequently roughed up by more worldly wise teams. We had called ourselves "Abbey St. Edmunds" and all our opponents knew that we were the local Church team. We were viewed as being oddities, softies and strange and other teams would treat us differently because of who we were. On one occasion we were playing away to the Junior Army team, The Royal Fusiliers. We were losing 4-0 at half time and we had taken a lot of stick and ribbing from a huge band of Army supporters. At this stage, we had lost all our previous matches quite heavily and were in danger of another bad defeat. At half time Fr. Minson took us to the centre of the pitch and reminded us of exactly who we were. He reminded us, as if he didn't need to, that we were "different," but that we had to behave sportingly and within the rules. However, he goaded us in no uncertain manner that we must have pride in ourselves, and pride in Abbey St. Edmunds and that we must go out for the second half and not be intimidated. He told us to show the Army Fusiliers just what we were made of. In the second half, we were like a team possessed. We took to the field and I scored three goals, my first hat-trick, with the game finishing 4-4. We very nearly won the game with a shot in the final minute and our pride was restored. I think that was the first time I had ever really felt someone special. We had been viewed as being the local oddities, the village idiots, and yet we had gone to the top team, come back from the dead and nearly beaten them. At last we had been proud of who we were. Yes, we were very different!

The education at the Juvenate was generally very good. It gave us a good classical training which was geared to the life we were planning to lead. It was not so good on practical subjects such as woodwork, science and the like, but it was to stand me in good stead. The class sizes were small, ranging from twelve boys at the age of eleven to just six by the time I was seventeen, and ready to take my Oxford GCE "O" Levels. I was a most definite slow starter but I benefited by the small class sizes, and the more personalised tutoring. When it came to exam time, I took the following subjects: English Literature, English Language, French, Latin, Geography, Religious Studies and History. I got pass marks in all seven subjects and had the distinction of being the only pupil not to have failed one subject! I did slightly cheat though, because whereas all the other boys sat the Mathematics GCE, my tutor did not put me in for it because I was so poor at Maths that he decided not to enter me for it. So what! I hated Maths, Algebra and anything to do with it, and I still do to this day. Thank Goodness for calculators and computers! Even so, I was more than ever pleased when Father Minson put a note on the school Notice Board saying as follows:

"Congratulations especially to Nearey, who has the distinction of being the only boy not to have failed a single Oxford G.C.E "O" Level" It was something of a back-handed compliment, but I was happy to get any compliments I could, and so I milked it for all it was worth by letting everyone know that I had passed them all.

In our last year at the Juvenate after our GCE O Levels, the pressure was off, in so far as the academic subjects had all been studied and the examinations had been completed. In the final year we had additional subjects such as Music, Spanish, Elocution and English Literature. The priest who usually taught us English Literature was taken ill and was to be unavailable for the best part of the year. As a result, Father Minson brought in an outside teacher to carry on with our English Literature classes. The new tutor was a middle aged lady called Miss Brinton, and while she was pleasant she was rather pompous and somewhat pretentious. On one occasion she gave us a task to do for homework. We were to do a critique of any famous novel to the class, with a famous author. One of the boys, Michael thought that he would play a prank on the teacher and he decided that he was going to call her bluff because he believed that she was a *"know it all"* and that she would fall for it. At English

Literature class it was Michael's turn to do his critique. Miss Brinton asked Michael which book and author he was going to critique: He replied: "I am going to critique **"London Nights"** by **Richard A. Brandon**. The problem was that there was no such book and no such author. Michael had invented the title and the name of the writer to see if the teacher would take the bait. We knew the true situation and waited with baited breath. Michael then did his critique to the class and then went a step further by asking Miss Brinton what she thought of the novel "London Nights" and its author. She replied as if she knew all about the book and that she knew of Richard. A. Brandon the author. *"London Nights is not one of my favourite books and I am not too keen on Brandon's writing style"* At this the class fell about laughing and the tutor did not have the slightest idea why! She asked the class why we were all laughing, but nobody had the courage or the stupidity to tell her the truth. I am sure that she would not have taken the prank lightly. It was a cruel trick to play, but after all, she had bluffed her way through it, so perhaps she deserved it after all. Talk about angelic schoolboys! I do not think so!

Eight

Holidays at Home

It was then the summer of 1965. We had broken up at the end of term in July and we had said our goodbyes to Matron, the tutors and our school friends. Along with all the other boys we left Erdington to go back to our respective families from all corners of the United Kingdom. As I travelled home, I wondered exactly which of us would return in September. Well who knows? Indeed, I did not know if I would be coming back to Erdington Abbey. Decisions by all of us would have to be made at some point in the not too distant future.

Going back home was great. Like all families, I missed my parents and my brothers and sister. I missed my Mum particularly. While I was in Birmingham she would write to me every week and I would post a letter in reply. There were, of course, no mobile phones and email in those days, and the art of letter writing was still an important one. Mum used to say that I always wrote interesting letters which were very 'newsy'. In fact, to day, my wife always says that although I am no use at D.I.Y, if there is one thing that I am good at, I can pen a good letter.

In fact it was the highlight of the week when Father Minson would bring the post round and as always, there was a letter from Mum. She hardly ever, if at all, went a week without writing to me. Dad also wrote to me, although less frequently. It was a work of art trying to decipher his writing anyway. His letters looked as if a spider had crawled into a pot of ink and then walked all over the page. His letters were short and to the point, usually one page in length, but at least he wrote. I was one of the lucky ones. Every single week I had my letter from Mum and about once a month there was one from Dad as well. Mum would always send me a postal order for my pocket money and I would invariably spend most of it on sweets. I often felt really sorry for some of my schoolmates. When the post arrived, there were one or two who never received any post at all and never received any money to spend. It was almost as if the boys had gone away and been practically forgotten by their families

Back in Manchester I was not the only one to return home. My elder Brother was also living away from home at a Seminary. He too was going to become a Priest although not in a Religious Order. He was training to become a Parish Priest. He was over two years older than me and he trained at St. Bede's College in Manchester, before going to a Seminary at Ushaw in County Durham. He was already back at home when I arrived. My younger Brother Mike also went to train with a Religious Order when he was thirteen, but he left and returned home for good after about two years. My Sister had gone away to train as a Housekeeper at Bath University. It was therefore quite a homecoming when we all arrived back at the family home during the summer months and it was quite a reunion. We were all in our mid-teens by then, and it was quite a strain on Mum and Dad having us all back at home once again. It was also a financial strain. Mum and Dad were never well off, and like most families from our type of background, their life was constantly a financial struggle.

So during our Summer Holidays, my Brother and I would obtain a temporary job as most students do to help the family finances. The previous year I worked for the local Council in Marple. In my fourth year I worked at the local swimming baths as an attendant. I was then given the job of inspecting every lamp-post within a five mile circumference of the town and doing a minor mechanical adjustment to each. And then in my fifth year, my summer job was working on the Dust Bins. This was quite a job but not one that I relished. I was a skinny kid, my nickname at school was 'Narrow' and I was not that strong. So it was quite a job to work on the Bins. In the sixties there were no pretty coloured Wheelie Bins on wheels filled with re-cycled paper and such-like. No, the bins were heavy metal ones, mostly filled with ash from coal fires. They were really heavy and I struggled to heave these across my shoulder and then manually tip them into the bin wagon. In the end, I think I must have been slowing down productivity because the foreman gave me the job of taking back the empty bins, but I did not complain.

At least I was seeing something of normal life during my summer holidays. In my fifth year of summer holidays, I got a summer vacation job at a local Mill just a couple of hundred yards from my home. In fact, it really was a family affair. Mum and Dad both worked there full-time. Mum was a Supervisor and Dad worked there too. Just like at home, Dad had to do as he was told by Mum! My elder brother was also working there. The Mill made foam 'flock' for the filling of cushions. Not the most exciting of jobs and it was dirty and noisy, but it was a living for my parents and it helped my brother and me to earn some money for ourselves and the family coffers during summer time. It didn't leave much time for enjoyment and recreation though. However, although known to the family, it did lead to a new development for me, girls!

It was a subject that had never been discussed either at home or at Erdington. Girls were never really mentioned and of course I was training to become a priest and monk, and that meant a celibate life in the Catholic Church. Even though at the age of fifteen, I was a normal healthy boy, I had never had any experience of girls other than as other human beings, and friends, but certainly not in any relationship way. So it came as quite a shock when I started to become friendly with a girl off the 'flocking' machine at The Goyt Cotton Mill in Marple. I was never confident as a youngster, always on the shy side, and I was not comfortable around girls. All my teenage years' to-date had been with Boys, and I just did not know how to handle this other species. They were somewhat different. Strangely, at Erdingon Abbey, our Art Teacher, Brother Alphonsus was at one time teaching us to draw the shapes of people. It was only in my fourth year that he drew the shapes of men and women and he explained the different shapes that we had. Until then it had never really dawned on me that men and women had such different body shapes. Perhaps I was just a very slow starter!

Back at the Goyt Mill I was quite friendly with this girl on the flocking machine. Her job was working the machine, and mine was to fill the boxes with flock and take them to the warehouse. At first I thought that it was just a friendly banter, until it gradually dawned on me that she quite liked me. Her name was Jill; she was sixteen, tall, pretty and very friendly and easy to approach. She needed to be because I was so awkward with girls and found it difficult to make small talk. Jill was a year older than me, but about twenty years older than me in experience and maturity. Slowly, she made it clear that she was not just being friendly and that she liked me a lot. It just started as we were chatting over the tea-break. It was just the two of us across a single table, and she started asking me questions about me. Until now, all the chat had been about work, the weather and everyday matters. She looked at me over a mug of hot tea and asked me about my family, where I lived and what I was doing at the factory. She knew I was not there full time and that it was a summer vacation job for me. For the first time, I was less than honest and I didn't really know why. I told Jill that I went to boarding school in Birmingham and that this was to be my final year there, when I returned in September. At one point she looked me directly in the eyes and asked me what I was going to do when I finished there. I hesitated, stumbled with my words and was clearly evasive. I said that I would wait and see how my examination results went and that I was undecided. I felt that there was going to be an awkward silence and then the factory hooter sounded for the end of the tea break and we went back to our work stations. Saved by the bell! As I went back to work I asked myself why for the first time, I had not been open and honest about my future and where I was going? Until that point, I had always told anyone who asked just what I was doing and where I was going. So, why was this situation suddenly very different? Even I did not know.

Later on that day I found myself thinking more and more about Jill. In fact, she was constantly on my mind. I found myself wondering close to where she worked so that I could talk to her. Suddenly, I couldn't get her out of my head. I started to think about her all the time. I would make excuses to find a reason to collect stock from where she was working. I had never felt this way before, but I was not going to do anything about it. I was too nervous, too shy, and anyway I would be going back to Erdington in about three short weeks, so what was the point?

5.30 pm arrived and the factory hooter sounded. Another day had finished. It was hard work on the flocking machines, and I was glad to be going home. After all, this was supposed to be my summer holidays. It was also Friday, the end of the week and I collected my wages of £6.20 for a forty hour week. It was not a lot, but at least I still had a bit of money jingling in my pocket after I had paid Mum for the housekeeping. I was leaving the building after collecting my pay packet, when Jill ran towards me as I was about to leave and said that she was going to have a party that night with a few friends and wondered if I would like to come? It took me completely by surprise. *"Errrr Yes"*, I blurted out. *"That would be great"*. Jill gave me a slip of paper with her address on it and said *"See you at 7.30pm"*. She only lived about half a mile from where I lived. I walked home, all of 250 yards, and with a feeling of shock and excitement that I had never experienced before. After all, I had never been out with a girl before, and somehow, it didn't seem quite right. I felt guilty, I felt scared, and yet I had a feeling of genuine excitement. Back home, it was the usual Friday night. We had all finished work, Mum Dad, and both my brothers and sister were home. That night, I quickly had a bath, spruced myself up and ate my tea. Mum had made one of her legendary cheese and onion pies. She knew I loved them, really heavy on the cheese and the onion!

After tea, I would normally do something with my brothers. Often, we would take a ball and go up-to the local recreation ground next to The Crown Public House and play football until dark. It was July, and it was daylight until about 10pm. So when my younger brother Mike suggested football on the Crown "Rec" I made an excuse and said that I was going for a drink with a couple of friends from work. Straight away he asked me if he could come with me as he was at a loose end that night. I made some really lame excuse about him not really liking these friends and I went out, shutting the door and shouting *"See you Later"*, *I may be late!!"* It was not like me at all. I was usually so straightforward and not evasive, and I felt sure that the family knew that I was up-to something! I got to Jill's house bang on 7.30pm, and tapped on the door. There was a lot of noise coming from inside. I could hear Hermans Hermits on the record player belting out *"How do you do what you do to me?"* After waiting for what seemed an age, Jill opened the door, the place was heaving. I did not think it was possible to get so many people into a small terraced council house. But despite there being so many friends there for what turned out to be her 19th birthday, she barely left my side all evening. It was just as well because I didn't know anybody else there at all, despite the fact that I lived so close by. It was not really surprising, as all my teenage years had been spent in Birmingham and even on holidays, I had never really mixed with any of the locals. It was like we were already an item, as Jill introduced me to all her friends, and stuck close to me all night. Around midnight, the time had just flown by; most of the friends were leaving. Jill stopped short of calling me her boyfriend, but she made it pretty clear that she wanted us to be an item and she was just waiting for me to take the initiative and ask her out. I must have been pretty useless because it was obvious that I was "smitten", but I did nothing to make the relationship firm. I gave her a peck on the side of the cheek, said that I had had a fabulous evening, and that I would speak to her at work on Monday. Talk about awkward. Maybe she thought I was playing it cool, or hard to get, or that I just did not fancy her. Nothing could have been further from the truth. I just could not get her out of my head, but I just did not know what to do. I was in foreign territory and I did not know which way to turn. I knew that I had told no lies, but neither had I been completely honest with her about anything. I didn't quite know how to, because I just did not know what I wanted to do, or what I should do. I wandered home on foot and crept in the front door. I was expecting the Spanish Inquisition. Usually the family were up and watching a late night horror film. But all was in darkness. My elder brother was in bed and my young brother and sister were still out on the town. Without making a sound I crept upstairs and slid into bed. I lay there thinking for a while! What was I going to do? It had been all very straightforward until now. In three weeks time I was going to go back to Erdington for my final year and then onto Perth to the Noviciate where I would become a Monk, and then to Hawkstone, to finally become a Priest. Then, all of a sudden, I had met Jill, completely out of the blue, at work, and for the first time, seriously, I just did not know what to do. I decided that the only course of action would be to sleep on it and see how I felt the following day. But whatever I decided upon, I had some explaining to do to Jill, and maybe to others.

I lay in bed that night and cursed my luck. Here I was, my life all neatly packaged and planned out and running very smoothly and then this happens. To tell the truth, girls had never really crossed my mind until then and I was reasonably happy and content at Erdington and I knew that I would be going onwards to Perth the following year. I had never missed having an experience with a girl because I had never had one, and what you haven't had, you generally do not miss! Then out of the blue this happens. The timing was all wrong as I began to feel things that I had never felt before. It was all out of the blue, and I just did not see it coming and was not expecting it. I just kept going over and over the memories of the fabulous night we had just experienced as I lay there trying to sleep. I was desperately trying to make some sort of sense of it all, but I had no idea what was going to happen next. I would never have dreamed that I would have met a girl like Jill and that she would have such an effect on me. It had just thrown all my plans and my well ordered life into absolute chaos. If I was to follow my heart and my feelings it would completely ruin my plans for my future life as a Priest, and if I followed my head then I would certainly miss out on the opportunity to be with a wonderful girl. Finally, tiredness got the better of me and before finally dropping off to sleep I came to the conclusion that I would wake up and find out that I would know precisely what I had to do.

The next morning arrived bang on time at 8am and the first thoughts that filled my head were the deliberations that I had grappled with the night before. It was Saturday and I still had no idea how I was going to resolve my dilemma. The hope that my sub-conscious mind would give me the answers to my deliberations overnight, was ill-founded and I was no nearer to making a decision. In such circumstances I had always gone along with the policy that if you do not know what to do, then it is best to do nothing. So that is precisely what I did. I still had the weekend to mull matters over and to give me more time to decide what to do next.

Nine

Decision Time

The new week came around so quickly. In fact the weekend just flew by and I was still filled with indecision. In just a few more days I was due to travel back to Erdington. I had finished my summer job of work at The Goyt Mill and I was preparing to leave home yet again. The family had no idea of my dilemma, as I had not spoken to any of them about it. Jill was working at the Mill that day and I arranged to meet her after work. We met at the coffee shop in town. She was excited when she arrived and began telling me about some plans for us to go out at the next weekend. I said *"Jill, I need to tell you something!"* I was nervous and it showed. But I continued *"I am going back to boarding school on Monday"*. She replied *"I know that, but we can see each other on the holidays, can't we?"* Finally, I just had to tell her. It was eating away at me and I just had to come clean. *"Jill, it is not just an ordinary boarding school I am at. I am training to become a Catholic Priest"*, I said apologetically. *"I am really, sorry but I just did not know how to tell you. I really like you very much"* I stumbled, *"and I just don't know what to do."* The look of shock on her face said it all. I just knew how she felt about me. The truth is, we were both smitten and we had strong feelings for one another. I tried to explain things to her, but none of it seemed to make any sense to her. I told her that I was going back to Erdington on Monday, but that I did not know what I would do after that. I said that I would go back and that I may decide at the end of next term when I came back home for Christmas with my family. It seemed the only thing that I could do. For all my strong feelings for Jill, I just knew at that stage, that I could not make any life changing decisions. With sadness, she seemed to accept what I had told her and she seemed to want to wait for me. We saw each other over the next weekend and we went to the cinema on Saturday afternoon and spent the evening together. On the Sunday, I had already made plans to do things with the family and I did not see Jill at all, but we had arranged to write to each other and maybe speak, when I got back to the Juvenate at Erdington.

Monday morning arrived and I had already packed and was ready to leave. Dad had already gone to work, but Mum was home and was helping me get all my things together. She could tell that I was not quite right that day. I had said nothing to her, but intuitively Mum could tell that I did not want to leave on that morning. She asked me if I was alright, and I said I was ok. I think Mum just thought that it was just normal that I did not want to go back to school after a long summer vacation and there was nothing more to it. Until that year, either Mum or Dad had come with me to the station, but I told her I was sixteen and that I would go on my own. I took the bus down to Marple Station and was waiting for my train to take me to Piccadilly Station in Manchester. It was early September and it was a lovely morning. I was sat on the station bench in the sunshine as I was about twenty minutes early for my train. I had always been one for being too early, rather than be late. I sat there deep in my thoughts. Yes, I was having genuine misgivings and uncertainty about where I was going and just what would happen next. I felt as if I was on a conveyor belt and I was being carried along but my feet were not moving. As I sat there in a world of my own, there was a tap on my shoulder. I turned, and to my pleasant surprise, it was Jill. She looked lovely, and her smile just lit up my day. *"I thought I would come and see you off"* she said. *"But I thought you were working today"* I replied. *"Well, I just took the day off today. I wanted to see you before you go."* Jill came with me on the train to Manchester. We talked and talked, but did not talk about anything too deeply, just small talk. All too quickly, we were at Manchester Piccadilly Station. We waited on Platform Two for the train to Birmingham. We had about fifteen minutes before the train left; it was a steam engine. As the time for departure drew near, the small talk dried up. Both of us were feeling nervous and tentative, neither of us knowing just what the future had in store. We held hands and kissed and then held each other. At the last moment, it was clear that the train was about to leave. The locomotive was belching out steam and sounding its whistle. The Guard was about to wave his green flag, and at the very last moment I jumped onto the train and wound down the window. *"You will write?"* Jill said. *"I promise",* I replied and with a heavy feeling and a knot in my stomach, we waved to each other until the platform and Jill were out of sight.

What was going to happen? Would I stay or would I go? The journey to Birmingham was horrible. I do not think that I even noticed the numerous blurred stations and landmarks as the steam train thundered along on its noisy journey to the Midlands. It was Jill that was on my mind during the entire journey. I had just left her on the station at Manchester but I wanted so much to be back with her and I knew that she wanted to be with me. It seemed to me that everybody I loved, whether it was my family, my friends and now Jill were being left behind and I wondered if and when I would see any of them again, and if I did, then would it ever be quite the same?

As the train got closer and closer to Birmingam, I realised that despite all my misgivings, I would be back at Erdington Abbey within a very short space of time. I knew that for the time being I had no choice that I could make. The time for that had now passed. The reality was that I would not be going back home to Marple until Christmas. In the circumstances I decided there and then that the only thing for me to do was to throw myself back into my life at Erdington and see how I felt after a week or two. As the train drew into the platform at Erdington station I took down my suitcase from the overhead rail and made my way to the carriage door. I walked slowly from the train station to Erdington Abbey as it was only a few hundred yards away. As I entered the large double gates to the Juvenate, Matron met me and said in her jolly Irish lilt: *"Did you have a good holiday then, Stephen?"*; *"What a Mess"* I thought to myself, but instead I replied: *"Yes Matron, it was wonderful, thank you."*

Ten

Sixth Form

The sixth form had finally arrived. It was September 1965. I had made it all the way to the top class at Erdington Abbey. The truth is that I never really believed that I would make it that far. I had not really felt confident in my own ability that I had what it took to be a scholar, a Monk and a Priest. I was just a kid from a council estate in Manchester. However, here I was, in year six at the Juvenate. I had arrived here as a pretty quiet young boy aged just eleven years old. Now I was actually still here at Erdington Abbey, still going ahead with the master-plan and I was now a 16 year old youth, with very little experience of life "outside", but becoming more and more experienced and engrossed in this totally different and unique life-style that I had chosen. I had achieved my educational goals so far and I had done rather better than anyone else expected, myself included. I was rather proud of my seven Oxford GCE "O" Levels. It began to become clear that the way ahead was different, because there was now no plan for me to take G.C.E. "A" levels. They were not necessary where I was going, as I would be taking a totally different educational route into academic subjects which are not normally related to our normal life style.

Was I totally convinced that the future that was mapped out for me was the correct one? The truth is; no it was not! Doubt and uncertainty had always been there. The fact that I had stayed at Erdington for over five years already was a testament to the fact that I enjoyed the life-style in many ways, even though I was very uncertain about the future years ahead. When I arrived at the Juvenate, there were twelve boys in my class. And already, coming into year six I was one of only five boys left in my class. Over the previous years, many of the boys had decided that this was not the life for them. In my first year at the Juvenate, there were boys from all walks of life. I was from a fairly typical working class background in the 1960's, but there were also boys from middle and upper class families who came, because they all had the same ideal. They all came because they believed, or were told, that they had been chosen. Yes, of course we had to accept our calling, but we ourselves did not choose it. We were the chosen ones. Although the Juvenate was a school of around sixty plus pupils, the fall out rate was very high. It was not a normal school and we bonded in a certain way. I suppose we could call it something of a siege mentality. I felt, for my part, that I was now a member of a much larger family. I had lived nearly six years of my young life away from my real family, except for school holidays. My school pals were more than that, and due to living together as well, I believed that we were all members of a close knit community. It was then, both difficult and sad when any of the boys, my friends, left the Juvenate. Normally, this would happen during the end of a term, when someone decided not to return as the new session began. I remember on more than one occasion that friends just did not return for the new semester, when I had been looking forward to seeing them again. It was very sad, a genuine feeling of loss. On other occasions, a boy would suddenly "disappear" during term. Either he or his parents had decided that the life was not for them, and all of a sudden, he would not be there anymore. It would happen whilst we were in class, or out for a walk, that one of the boys would have his bags packed and would be taken to the train station or collected by his parents without speaking to us or saying goodbye. It felt to me as if there was something underhand about the ways boys would leave. It seemed that once somebody had decided to return to outside life, they were cut-off and moved out very quickly. One of the Priests would just tell us that such a boy had decided to leave, and that was the end of that. I think perhaps that they believed it would be less upsetting than having to say a fond goodbye. It happened to me on two occasions that friends of mine just left the Juvenate during term and I had no understanding of the reasons why, and after that, there was no further contact with them. I found this very difficult to deal with. Perhaps it was done with good intentions of not upsetting friends and having to deal with questions as to why they had left. It was very upsetting; however, it did reinforce the view that those who remained were indeed, "the chosen ones".

The last year at Erdington was a year of decision making. For the first few days back at Birmingam, Jill was on my mind all the time. I felt really unsettled and was really unsure about why I was still there when I felt that I wanted to be back at home. Yes, I missed my family a lot and I missed life at home, but now I was also missing Jill and she was in my mind for much of the time. This was September 1965 and mobile phones had not been invented, neither had the internet so contact was by letter post. After I had been back a couple of days I wrote to Jill and told her I was missing her, but I was unable to tell her what would happen in the near future. There was too much involved and the decision to stay or go was just too big for me to handle at that stage. There were too many people involved who would feel hurt one way or the other and I felt that I had to consider them too. My parents paid for me to go to Erdington. Our family was not well off and like many working class families at that time, money was always short, so I really appreciated the fact that they worked overtime, and scrimped and saved, to pay for me to go to the Juvenate and to live the live that I had chosen. Jill and I continued to exchange letters for the first few weeks and she kept telling me that Christmas was not too far away, and that we could see each other again.

Weeks passed, and I became involved in life back at Erdington. It was always very busy. We had a very full day, every day and the whole week seemed to pass by very quickly. We had lessons, jobs, prayers, services, sport, and a very full schedule every day and at weekends and little by little, I became more settled again. Boarding school was a great life in many ways and I had my friends. We played football most of the spare time we had, and although we continued to exchange letters, Jill's correspondence became more like that of a friend or mate, rather than a girlfriend. By the end of November, her letters became less frequent, and then I received a letter from her telling me that she was seeing a lad at the factory but that she wanted to remain good friends with me. I suppose it was bound to happen. I had become engrossed again in life at boarding school and in my letters I had given her no encouragement that the situation was going to change anytime soon. In some ways it was a relief, because it had resolved a difficult and emotional situation for us both, at least for the time being. I did see Jill one last time at Christmas. I called to see her when I went home for the holidays. When I saw her, it just felt different. She felt just like a friend now and we chatted and I told her about what I was doing at Erdington. In fact, it was just as well. Jill had been seeing this other guy for some weeks. She seemed keen on him and it seemed as if she had got over me too. I don't really believe in fate, but at that time, that's exactly what it felt like.

My final year at Erdington was a strange one, like treading water. I had done all my GCE O Levels, and then normally, the next step for me and the others, would be to take GCE A Level courses and then examinations. However, at this stage we no longer needed to continue with the subjects we had taken, because in just a few short months I would be studying a totally different syllabus, when I would move onto the Noviciate at Perth and then onwards a year later, to the Hawkstone Seminary.

In my final year at Erdington, the emphasis was very much on preparation for moving onto the Noviciate in Perth in September of 1966. Life had changed quite considerably over the years since I came to Erdington in 1960. At that time, we had twelve boys in the class, and here I was in year six and I was just one of six boys remaining, a fifty per cent drop out rate. This was difficult to deal with and I surprised myself that I was still one of the remaining six. There were other boys that I felt certain would continue, and yet they had gone. It had not been an easy journey. I was never the best of pupils in terms of ability, but I was very much a late developer. As the years progressed I became better and better, and no doubt, much of it was due to the small class size, but I also developed as a pupil, studied hard and was determined to succeed. The tutors were able to give us a much more personal and thorough teaching and a good grounding for the years ahead. Instead of normal studies, we concentrated much more on learning about the life in the Noviciate. The nearer it came to the date for moving there, the more nervous some of my school-mates became, and we were to lose another two boys before the end of my final term in the spring of 1966. By the end of that term, the twelve boys I had started with in 1960 had now become just four. I wondered if I too, would last the final term, and if I would ever get to go to the Noviciate in Perth. In those final months of that year, our studies were not about the normal subjects of Maths and English and such like, and our lessons concentrated on preparing us for the life of a Novice. I was filled with self doubt. Did I want to continue? Why had so many of my friends and colleagues left and decided not to continue with the life? The fact that so many had departed put even more pressure on me to stay the course and become a Monk and then a Priest. The assumption by everybody, my family and everyone at Erdington, was that I would continue on the path I had "chosen". I was just seventeen years old. I was not sure if I had chosen anything at all. I had an inner feeling that it had all just happened, that I had just been carried along by the inevitable process that had begun in 1959. That was when I visited the exhibition of Religious Orders and found myself making a decision about a whole new life at the grand old age of eleven years. I was not sure about much, but one thing I knew for sure, was that I was expected to continue there. This put unenviable pressure onto me. I was grateful to my family, especially my parents, but also to everyone at Erdington who had helped me to get to this stage. If I left Erdington and went back to what we call "normal" life, what would I do? Also, I did not want to hurt my parents and my tutors at Erdington. They had invested a lot of time and years in me, and had seen so many boys fall by the wayside. They were really proud of me, and they really would have been proud if I continued on to become a Priest. On the other hand, I knew they would be upset and greatly disappointed if I too decided to leave. No pressure then! Thank goodness, I did not have to make that decision until the end of term in June 1966; I still had a few months in which to decide.

The final term was quite surreal at Erdington. There were just *"the gang of four"* left in the sixth form from the twelve that had started as young boys in 1960. We were now realising that life was soon about to change for us, if we decided to move to the Noviciate at Perth in September. Naturally, we talked among ourselves a lot and the other three boys had the same doubts and fears that I did, so at least I was not alone on that score. The weeks passed by quickly, and most of our discussions with the priests and tutors were about our impending move to Perth. So far, there had just been a tacit but unspoken assumption that we would continue to the Noviciate, but in June 1966 I was called into The Juvenate Director's office. *"Well Stephen,* he said: *"You've been here six years now, and we will miss you very much. You have been an excellent pupil, but it is time now for you to move onto your next stage at the Noviciate in Perth. Are you looking forward to it?* The directness of the question shocked me greatly. I was not expecting it at all. I was surprised and taken aback. I had expected that there would have been at least a discussion about my future and that I would then have made a decision after I had time to consider it. But no, it was a "fait-accomplit" He asked me if I was looking forward to going to the Noviciate at Perth. I must have looked shocked! I did not answer at first, and he asked me again: *"Are you looking forward to it?"* Without further hesitation I blurted out: *"Yes, I'm very excited about going to the Noviciate".* As soon as I had said the words, I was filled with self-doubt, and I could not believe what I had just agreed to, but I did not let it show. I don't know why I did so. On the one hand I was really nervous about what I had just signed up to. On the other hand, it was, after all, what I had been training for during the past six years and I was genuinely excited about it. The Juvenate Director went on to tell me what was going to happen and gave me all the information about the move to my new home in Scotland. For the second time, I had made a life changing decision in an instant, and I was both frightened and excited at the same time. Only time would tell if I was right to move to Perth.

Saying goodbye to The Juvenate and Erdington was a huge wrench. I had spent all my teenage years in this unusual place and I had grown a genuine attachment to it. It was a Monastery and also a boarding school and it had been my home for six years. All my friends were there and I had no other friends outside of it. Saying goodbye to all my friends was terrible, even though I knew that four of them were also planning to come with me to Perth. As I left on 30th June to go to the Railway Station, I felt that I was leaving behind the only life style I had known, and I was genuinely nervous about the life that lay ahead.

Going back home to my family in Marple gave me a good feeling. It was a strange feeling though, as I was coming home from an institution for just six weeks, to my loving family home, and then I would be going to go to an even greater institution on 1st. September of that year.

The summer months were unusual to say the least. It was a period where normality was to be short lived. It was as if I was in Limbo. In Catholic Theology, Limbo refers to states of oblivion, confinement or transition. It is derived from the theological sense of Limbo as a place where souls remain that cannot enter heaven, for example un-baptized infants. The teaching was that only the baptized can enter Heaven. On the other side of course is Hell. So to be in Limbo was like being in "No Man's Land". That is exactly how I felt at that moment in time. I was between the devil and the deep blue sea, unsure which way to go.

The summer of '66 was indeed an iconic year. England won the World Cup, and it was a long hot summer at home. I started work on a part-time job with the local council again. Money was always tight at home and we all had to contribute when we could. In some ways, getting a job seemed quite normal. I was a part-time swimming pool attendant at the local swimming baths, and then I was given a job changing the timing clocks on every lamp-post in the town. Normality reigned, at least for a while, but it was as if I was treading water. My elder brother had also taken the path to becoming a Catholic Parish Priest. He too had been away at boarding school, and he had now progressed to a senior seminary and was two years ahead of me. It was strange, but we very rarely spoke about our futures to each other. We just continued along the path and did our own thing and in our own different ways

All too quickly, the summer of 1966 was over. No sooner had I arrived home from Erdington for my six week summer vacation, and then it was finished. I had worked hard at my job for the local Council for most of the six weeks and the time just seemed to fly by. The days were becoming cooler and wetter. England were the World Cup Champions, and the time had come for me to move on to the next stage of my young life. Arrangements had been made for me to go to Perth, at the Redemptorist Noviciate. I had received a letter from the Novice Master giving me details about going to live at the Noviciate in Perth. It told me what to take, and what not to take with me, and the arrangements for arriving there on 1st.September that year. I had been put in touch with another new boy, John Hirst, who lived just a few miles from my home in Hyde Greater Manchester. He had not been at Erdington with me and had arrived at his decision to join the Religious Order by an entirely different route to mine. My family did not have a car and so we arranged to travel together to Perth in their family vehicle which was an estate car and could take six passengers and all of our suitcases.

Eleven

The Noviciate

The car arrived at the front door of my house at Marple. My suitcase was packed. John Hirst and his Father came to help me with my cases, but considering that I was about to move home permanently, it seemed that I had very few possessions to take with me. I had just one suitcase and a small shoulder bag. The only things I took with me were my clothes. I took underwear, socks, shirts sweaters and trousers. I would not need any suits or coats as these, and all my other needs, were to be provided by the Noviciate.

It was a tiring seven hour journey from Marple to Perth covering some three hundred miles. The motorway system of today was not in place then, and we took a mixture of trunk roads along with A and B roads up through England and onto the east coast of Scotland. I had never been north of the border before and was fascinated by the beautiful and dramatic scenery on the long journey north. I travelled with my new friend John, his Father and my own Mother and Father. It was a strangely quiet journey, and after chatting for the first hour or so, not much was said for the remainder of the time. That was not just due to the length of the travel, but because of the circumstances. There was a definite feeling of apprehension on my part and John's, and no doubt our families were also feeling the impending separation from their sons. After all, I was going to live in a Monastery for a full year, during which time there would be no physical visits and very minimal telephone and letter contact. I sat in the rear of the car, just looking out of the window, occasionally nodding off into slumber, and then waking to admire the dramatic mountains and wonderful scenery that lay before us. We just passed occasional comments about the places of interest that we saw out of the car window but it was a very subdued atmosphere. Strangely, very little was said about the place we were going to, and small talk was the order of the day.

We journeyed through Edinburgh, marvelling at the sights, the castle and the surrounding rivers and lakes. If that was dramatic, then the drive over the Forth Road Bridge was even more so. As we reached Fife on the other side of the bridge, the rolling hills, mountains and scenery were breathtaking. We were now quite close to Perth. As we slowly approached the town via the winding country roads, there was a sense of anticipation, if not anxiety, in all of us. We passed through the centre of Perth and were now very close to our destination. Perth was a bit of a disappointment. After the dramatic sights of Edinburgh, the town was a very dull and dour place. The buildings were old, grey and very foreboding. No doubt the grey low mist and the constant drizzling rain added to the feeling of a cold dour Scottish town. Suddenly, we were out of the centre and heading up a very steep incline called Kinnoull Hill. I recognised this as being part of the address. We drove slowly up the hill and reached the top. There was a steep cliff face in front of us. We could not see our destination, but we were met by a panoramic view many hundred's of feet below and overlooking the winding River Tay and the Tay Valley. We stopped to ask directions from a local man out walking his dogs. As we asked him for travel directions to St.Mary's Monastery, Kinnoull Hill, he gave us a wary look and then pointed us in the general direction with his stick, with only brisk and brusque instructions. Only later were we to find out that many of the locals in Perth treated the Monastery with some suspicion. Perth was a largely Protestant and religious town and the Catholic Monastery on Kinnoull Hill, was something of a curiosity to some of the locals.

Within a couple of minutes, the car had pulled in through the large imposing gates and into the grounds of the Monastery. We were met by a very large and imposing structure. St. Mary's, Kinnoull had been built around 1850, in a commanding style which was both beautiful and intimidating at the same time. This was the home of the Redemptorist Monks and Missionaries in Scotland. It was also the home of the Noviciate. This was to be the place where novice monks would live for a full year to find out if this was to be the life for them, or perhaps not.

With some trepidation I took it upon myself to knock on the two very large wooden doors before realising that there was a large rope bell, which I then pulled. I could hear the bell clang inside of the building. John and our family then joined me on the steps with the suitcases. We waited quite some time before the door was opened. I was dressed smartly in a dark suit, white shirt and bright flowery tie. It crossed my mind that I would not dress like this again for quite some time. As the doors opened we were greeted by an elderly Monk with a cheery disposition who took us all inside and then asked us to sit down in what appeared to be a stark white waiting room. It was decorated very demurely with just a few chairs and a very large wooden mahogany table scattered with religious magazines. After leaving us for several minutes he then returned with a huge metal tea urn which had seen better days, and rich tea biscuits. *"You'll be tired after your journey?"* he said: in a broad Scottish accent *"You won't be getting biscuits every day"* he told us with a laugh. *"They are normally just for the visitors! Please enjoy your tea and have a wee rest."* He then told us that the Novice Master would come to see us very shortly.

After about fifteen minutes, and what seemed to be an eternity, we had just about exhausted all the small talk we had. We sat there nervously waiting for what was to happen next. Suddenly, in breezed The Novice Master. He was tall, quite thin and looked rather stern. He introduced himself to all the family, quite politely, but with a reserve that may have seemed like a lack of warmth. Initially he spoke to our parents and told them he would give them a tour of the public rooms and gardens before their journey home. This he did and then we all returned to the waiting room where we had taken tea. *"Well Now"* The Novice Master said to the family: *"The boys will want to get themselves settled in and I'm sure that you have a long journey home so I'll leave you to say your goodbyes."* He then left the room and said that he would be back shortly.
John and I were both nervous as we started to say goodbye to his father and to my parents. We were almost adults: I was just 17 days short of my eighteenth birthday and John a little younger. However, we were still boys in many ways and it was a wrench to say farewell to our

parents. At Erdington I was away from home for most of the year but I returned to my family at the end of each term for quite lengthy holidays. Here the situation was something entirely different. We were to be Novices, a long way from home, for a full year and would not see our parents again during that time and there was to be very minimal contact, and that only by letter. It suddenly all felt very final. Of course, I kept a stiff upper lip, and did not let them see my true feelings. That's how we had been taught and brought up. We kissed and hugged on the front steps and there were tears in my Mother's eyes as she got back into their car for another very long journey home. We waved until they disappeared out of sight at the end of the drive and then we slowly went back inside the Monastery. We sat with our suitcases for a few moments wondering what was going to happen next. Within a couple of minutes the Novice Master returned and said: *"Right now Brothers! Welcome to St. Marys Monastery, let's get you settled in."* It was to be the true start of a long, often difficult but momentous journey.

It felt straight away that it was going to be an entirely new experience to what we had been used to at Erdington and while the Priests at the Juvenate had done their level best to prepare us for the coming year, I had a feeling that there was going to be a massive culture shock to the new Novices who had just arrived at Perth. I picked up my solitary suitcase and glanced one more time at the outside. It was early September in the late afternoon and dusk was fast approaching. Our parent's vehicles had all disappeared out of site down the end of the drive and they were on their way back to their homes from all parts of the

United Kingdom. We were not to see them again for another long year, except for those that were to leave the Noviciate before the year was up. It all seemed very final.

All the new Novices [known at that stage as Postulants] were stood around in the visitor's room, suitcases by their side waiting for the Novice Master to show them to the cell that had been allocated to them. It seemed that we all felt rather lost and unsure about ourselves. It was a massive life changing decision we had all made, and we seemed to be quiet and tentative as we waited to see what would happen next. It was all so new and such a huge change to anything that we had previously experienced. The Novice Master had decided to show just two at a time to their new living quarters. As I waited my turn to go inside, I felt more nervous than at any other time of my life. I just stood there, perhaps twiddling my thumbs and trying to make small talk with the other Postulants, but it did not come naturally. Then, all of a sudden the Novice Master breezed back into the visitor's room. He said in a softly spoken but decisive voice: *"Stephen and John", let me show you to your cells"*

Twelve

Day One as a Novice

As we entered the Monastery I experienced the strangest of experiences. I wondered what I was doing there. I had chosen to do so, but I was there because during the past six years of my boyhood, this is what I had trained for. I had feelings of anxiety and anticipation mixed with a fair amount of fear. It all seemed so strangely surreal. The Novice Master led the way deep into the bowels of the Monastery. Suddenly, although this was September 1966, I had the strangest feelings that it could have been 1866 or even 1766. The emotion of going backwards in time was very real. I was stepping into a world of yesteryear. The monastic life had clung onto its traditions and ways. On the outside it was the new modern world, and yet on the inside we were still in a previous century. The Novice Master marched briskly in front, along wide hollow empty cloisters that echoed with every step of his steel capped shoes on the stone floors. John and I followed behind, suitcases in hand. There was a feeling of quiet and serenity all around. As we walked, we cast fleeting glances at the statues of Mary and the Saints that seemed to be in every section of the building. Although it had been constructed in 1850, it somehow seemed much, much older than that, and steeped in a history that had unfolded during 2000 years. After walking around the cloisters for what seemed an age, we began to climb the steps up-to the second, third and finally the fourth floors. With each floor we climbed, the steps became steeper and narrower with the shiny stone slabs showing many, many years of wear and tear. Eventually, we arrived on the fourth floor. It was quickly apparent that we were on the top floor of the monastery and that it was in the roof-space of the attic. From being wide open cloisters with high ceilings, the fourth floor became narrow, cramped and with low ceilings that seemed somewhat oppressive. At the very end of the corridor on the east wing, the Novice Master stopped. *"Brother Stephen"* he said: *"This is to be your cell"*. The words had a chill all of their own. My only understanding of the word cell was that of a prison, a place of confinement and at first glance, that was precisely what it felt like. I was to understand later that "cell" in monastic parlance meant a room or unit.

I walked into my cell, casting furtive glances at what were to be my new surroundings for the coming year. It would not take long; the room was no more than eight feet by six. The ceiling was very low and sloped even lower at one end. There was a single attic window which although small, it gave sufficient light. On a positive note we were high up and the glorious view over the gardens and looking down over Perth, were enough to give me the feeling that there was still a world out there that I knew and recognised. The Novice Master suggested that I unpacked my belongings and told me that he would be back after he had showed John to his own cell.

Suddenly, I was alone for the first time. I just stood in my cell, put the suitcase onto my bed and surveyed my surroundings. It was furnished very sparsely. The wooden floor creaked with every movement I made. The bed looked as if it had seen years of service and had a thin striped mattress with thin white cotton sheets and a thick over-blanket. That was going to be necessary in a cold and damp monastery in the east of Scotland. The bedstead was of wrought iron construction and was clearly many years old. On the bed were a simple wooden crucifix and a copy of the bible. The bed barely fitted the length of the room. On the other side were a simple square table and chair made of real mahogany, and in the corner was a small wardrobe. A single light bulb with no shade hung from the ceiling. There was no heating of any kind in the room, although there was an ancient form of water heating that ran through the corridors and clanged loudly every time the system fired up, which was not very frequently.

On the table in my cell, were a very large white ceramic bowl and a huge jug. This was to be my main method of washing, accompanied by a large tablet of carbolic style soap. There was no running water to the room. Neither was there a mirror in my cell which made shaving quite a challenge. Mirrors were frowned upon and not provided, as they were deemed to be a form of vanity and were to be avoided unless absolutely necessary. As a compromise to cleanliness, [teaching has it, that cleanliness is next to godliness!], there was a single bathroom and toilet at the far end of the corridor which was shared between ten cells. It did have a bath, although the availability of warm, not to mention hot water, was very limited and infrequent, dependant upon the clanking old heating system. There was a rota for having a bath, which was pinned on to the door. At least it prevented queuing. It was such a long walk in the depths of the night to use the toilet that a white enamel chamber pot was provided for that very purpose.

As I stood gazing into nothing, still endeavouring to come to terms with my new surroundings, the Novice Master entered again. After a long wearisome journey, which had taken much of the day, it was now approaching 7pm and I was feeling very tired and hungry. He told me that supper was being served in the refectory. We descended onto the ground floor into a large room furnished with heavy wooden tables and chairs. The Novice Master showed me where I was to sit. In the centre of the room was a lectern which was for the purpose of providing readings and prayers. The bell clanged five times. It vibrated and echoed throughout the monastery. This was the call to the Monks to come to the refectory [dining room], for supper. Within moments around thirty Monks arrived and took to their own designated places at the tables. This all happened in silence and not a word was uttered. Mingled around the tables were the twelve new Novices. It was obvious to everyone, as to which were the Novices as we were all still dressed in outside attire, mainly of dark suit and tie with a white shirt. The thirty or so Monks, Brothers and Priests were dressed in monastic garb, depending on their status, but all with the familiar black Redemptorist habit, a full length robe, with white collar and belt, from which hung a huge set of rosary beads. The Rector arrived in the room and everybody stood. There was a varied collection of people in the room. At one end of the spectrum there were very elderly Monks who may well have been there for fifty years or more. There were Priests and Brothers along with the previous intake of Novices who were due to go to Hawkstone in just a few days time. At the other end of the spectrum, there were the fresh faced Novices, [known as Postulants for the first four weeks], most of which were just eighteen years old or thereabouts. One of the new Brothers that had arrived here with us that day was just fifteen years of age.

The Rector briefly addressed the monks and welcomed the newly arrived Novices to their new home at Perth. *"Fathers, Brothers!"* he said, as his quietly spoken voice echoed around the refectory, *"I wish to welcome all our new Novices to St. Mary's at Perth, I am sure that you will do all that you can to make them feel welcome and at home. Tonight there will be no readings during supper and we will have free association."* This meant that we could speak during the meal.

Meals were nearly always taken in silence, but in order to meet all our fellow Monks and Brothers on this first day, we were permitted to talk. The Rector said Grace: *"Bless us Oh Lord, for these thy gifts, which we about to receive, and May the Lord make us eternally grateful, Amen"* At this, the room broke into a controlled low hum of noise as the Novices chatted nervously to their elder Monks and Brothers. The main meal of the day was always at 12 noon and supper at 7.30pm, was a simple affair. This was served by Brothers who waited on the others and had their meal afterwards. Supper was a thick vegetable soup, served with large chunks of crusty bread which were baked in the Monastery kitchens. It was wholesome and filling and was accompanied by a glass of dark beer. This was a tradition that went back many years, although the beer was not brewed by the Monks. After the soup a desert of rice and jam was served and the meal was done.

At 8.30pm, and after supper, we all moved en-bloc to the recreation room. This was normally the only time of day that all the brothers and monks congregated together for a social gathering. The recreation room was furnished simply but it was comfortable. It was a place for quiet relaxation and communication. In the corner was an old radio, but it was rarely used and crackled too much. There was a selection of straight-backed and some comfy chairs, which were reserved for the older monks. Some sat and started making various crafts, whilst others would read magazines or books, but in the main, they gathered in small groups and spoke to each other. We were soon to learn that this in itself was very important, as for much of the day, work and duties were carried out in silence.

As 9.30pm approached, a bell rang again, and this time it was to usher the Monks to evening prayer. Quietly, [everybody stopped speaking], we all moved to the chapel where evening prayers were said: This consisted of various chants and prayers of thanksgiving for the day just finishing. At 9.45pm, we all returned in silence to our cells, where I washed and got dressed for bed. I looked around the bare basic room and the thought crossed my mind that this was to be my home for the next year. I then climbed into my bed which creaked as I lay on it. I wondered about what other people had also laid on this same bed, and what had become of them. Had they gone on to become Monks? I wondered if anybody had died in that same bed. I quietly admonished myself for having stupid thoughts and then put it out of my mind. I felt completely out of my comfort zone. Everything was so different and new. I felt really uncomfortable and ill at ease. I had been told in advance what kind of lifestyle to expect at Perth but the reality was something entirely different. It was as if we had gone back in time to another time zone and already, on my very first day, I was feeling very unsure about the wisdom of coming to the Noviciate. Perhaps it was just first day nerves and maybe tomorrow I would feel completely different. Perhaps if I had a good night's sleep I would wake up the next day and have a totally different complexion about my new life.

I tried very hard to relax and hoped that I would soon drop off to sleep. I was so tired after the long journey and the events of the day that my mind was still in overdrive. I imagined that I could have lain awake all night trying to make sense of it all. As it was, I was so tired that I tried hard to just clear my mind completely and drop off to sleep. Despite my best efforts though, I lay staring at the ceiling wondering what time it was and unable to sleep. I had no watch and no clock and I could only guess at the time by the light coming into the room. I had left my curtains wide open and light was streaming into my cell. I got out of bed and went to the window. The moon was large and full and seemed to give off a brilliant glow. Despite that, the night sky was awash with stars. I gazed out in wonder at the sky which was littered by millions of stars and planets which seemed to be clustered together in large groups. By comparison our tiny earth was miniscule and insignificant. In the countryside there were very few streetlights and other than the stars and the moon, darkness prevailed. As I gazed out at this night-time light show, I began to wonder about the universe, about how life had come into existence and about what it all meant. It was hard to make any sense of it all and the only way I could do so was for me to believe in God, because nobody else had the answers to the many questions that the solar system posed. As my mind kept marvelling at the universe in front of me I began to wonder about the maker of the solar system and what an amazing spectacle it all was. I could have stood there in the cold and dark for hours just being amazed at what I was seeing before me, but my body was cold and mind was so tired that I could barely keep my eyes open and my mind operating. I still had no idea of the time, but I knew that every action at the Monastery was dictated by the bell, so I did not worry any more about it. I knew that I would get up when the bell tolled. I just climbed back into my cold bed, tried to make it as comfortable as I could and eventually my sleepy head sank into the pillow and gradually I sloped off into a temporary oblivion.

Thirteen

First Full Day

The next day dawned with a sudden start at 5.30am. One of the brothers marched down the cloister knocking on every door as he went along. He was clearly the official "knocker-upper" and as he knocked on each door he chanted: "Gaudete" the Latin for "Rejoice". I responded with the same word. Try as I may, I did not feel much like rejoicing at that time on a chill September morning in Scotland. Immediately I fell to my knees by the side of the bed. This had been the norm for six years at Erdington, so I was well practiced. I muttered a few words in prayer to myself and then started to get ready. Morning Prayer [Matins] was at 6am, so I needed to move quickly. For an instant as I threw back the bed covers, I was unsure just where I was, but quickly as I got to my feet, I remembered, and my first thought was the wish that I was back at home. Still, I had no time to dwell on such thoughts. Using the white jug I poured cold water into the sink and began to shave. I had never had to shave in cold water before and as the cold blade pulled across my face it cut me and I began to bleed. I had no time to waste so I quickly covered the cut with tissue and washed and dressed. This was all completed on auto-pilot, so I cannot have looked my best, still as long as I was presentable then it sufficed. Hurriedly, I made my bed and tidied my cell and it was time to go to chapel. The bell sounded and I moved quickly along the cloister. As I did so, other Monks and Novices came quietly out of their cells and walked softly and in absolute silence towards the chapel. I took my place in my designated pew. We were always to go to exactly the same place. For no particular reason I could fathom, every monk had their own specific place, whether it was in the chapel, the refectory or the common room. It was perhaps the only piece of ownership they were ever to have. At 6.00am, all the monks were in their pews at the chapel, and so started thirty minutes of meditation. We had not as yet been taught anything about meditation, other than what we had learned at the Juvenate, so for the time being, I just made it up as I went along. The idea was to meditate about God, about life, and particularly, our own life. For what seemed an age I thought about God and about why I was here in Perth, and about how I hoped to spend the rest of my life. At times my mind wondered, and I felt guilty for doing so. Instead of concentrating on the meaning of my life, my thoughts wondered as to what we were going to have for breakfast, and other un-godly things of little consequence. Quickly I would correct myself and concentrate on my meditation. Occasionally, head in hands, kneeling in my pew, it was easy to move from meditation to drowsiness and almost fall asleep. I glanced around at my brothers, all with eyes shut, leaning on their pew, deep in meditation, or were they? I wondered if all the others were the same as me.

After thirty minutes of meditation, at 6.30 each morning, Mass would be celebrated, and it would be the same ritual each and every day, with just slight variations depending on the time of year and the relevant feast day. Mass is the Catholic celebration of the Eucharist where bread and wine are turned into the body and blood of Christ. This is the central belief of Catholicism, and it is a service that we would carry out religiously every day of our lives. Ever since the early days of the Roman Empire, the Mass was carried out in Latin. Fortunately, I had studied Latin for six years at the Juvenate, and although Latin is now a "dead" language, [nobody speaks it anymore], understanding it was a benefit, as the Catholic Mass was always said in Latin back in the 1960's. Even so, it was strange serving Mass in Latin, even though we had learned the text and I knew it by heart. Each day, we would attend Mass and often serve and assist the Priest as he celebrated it. One day, that might be me, and for all the Novices, this was the goal that we were to strive towards.

It was now 7am, Meditation and Mass were completed and we moved quickly and silently onto breakfast. The meaning of "breakfast" was indeed to break one's "fast". It was a key part of our rule that after supper and until breakfast, nothing at all was eaten and nothing was spoken. This was known as the "great silence". Even so, from supper at 7.30pm until breakfast at 7am was almost twelve hours and I had not been used to that length of time without eating at least something. At the Juvenate or at home, with the healthy appetite of any teenager, I would have food or snacks late into the evening, but fasting was a regular feature of the monastic life.

At the end of Mass, we had all walked without speaking to the refectory where breakfast was to be taken. Mornings were silent in the main, unless it was absolutely necessary to speak. I took my place at the breakfast table. On it was a big urn of thick porridge, and the obligatory Kelloggs

Cornflakes. This never varied, and the big decision of every morning was to decide: porridge or cornflakes! For me it was a "no brainer". The porridge was made in true Scottish tradition, thick and lumpy with water and salt! Ugh! I tried it on day one, and thereafter it was Kelloggs Cornflakes for a full year. The cereal over, there were bread rolls and coffee. During this, not a word was spoken by anybody except for the reader, who would mount a pulpit in the breakfast room and read to the Monks while they ate their meal. He would have to take his breakfast later on. The Monks took it in turn to be the reader for that particular day. At this breakfast meal, it was usually a classical book about the lives of one of the Saints, something that was meant to inspire us all during the day.

When breakfast was over, the daily routine was to continue. The golden rule was that silence was the order of the day, until after lunch, at recreation time. By that, it meant that normal conversation or chit chat were generally forbidden unless absolutely necessary. If for example I passed another Monk in the cloister, it would be appropriate to nod to him in polite acknowledgment, but it was forbidden to stop and chat about unnecessary matters.

Immediately that breakfast was completed at 7.30am, the Novices then went about the task of our morning chores. This involved the full daily cleaning of the Monastery. This was done entirely by the Monks and Novices. Each was allocated a task for a period of one month and then these jobs would change in rotation every four weeks. My first morning job was to clean and tidy my own cell, and then to thoroughly clean the cloister on the top floor where the Novices cells were situated. Cleaning my own cell was no problem as it was so small and had barely any furniture and possessions in it anyway, so two minutes and the job was done. The Cloister was a bigger job of work, requiring mopping, dusting and polishing a one hundred yard and eight foot wide floor, but after half an hour it sparkled and it was time to move onto other things.

At last, there was a little breather, and a bit of time to myself. Prayers had been said, breakfast was completed and morning chores were out of the way for the present. I had an hour to consider what had happened to me so far and to ponder just what was to happen next. I wanted to clear my head, and so I went outside the monastery for the first time since I had arrived. It had been a crisp, cold September morning and there had been a ground frost. At the rear of the building, the monastery looked imposing and proud. It stood close to the top of Kinnoull Hill and peered out over the dramatic hills and countryside of Perthshire. The newly cut lawns were crisp and manicured, and with a ground frost shimmering white, they were pristine in appearance. The sense of peace and tranquillity were almost tangible, save for the occasional twitter of birds making their early morning appearance and searching frantically for food. I wandered into the grounds, along the crunching gravel paths, taking deep breaths of clean fresh Scottish air deep into my lungs. It made me feel calm and refreshed on that first morning. The past day I had felt tense and anxious due to the newness of this extraordinary new life, this new journey that I had just embarked on. As I walked around I felt a brief feeling of inner calm. The skies were clear, and the sun had put in an early morning appearance low in the northern sky, making me feel good to be alive. The secluded gardens were a thing of beauty and the trees were golden with various colours of red as they began to take on their autumnal appearance. As I turned a corner into the wooded area of the garden, I came upon a statue of St. Alphonsus in a secluded area. I stopped a while to admire it and whilst I did this, an elderly brother came by. He too was taking an early morning constitutional, but I did not know his name. My immediate reaction was to say *"Good Morning, Brother!"* which I blurted out in a cheery tone. I had completely forgotten the morning rule of silence. He glanced briefly at me, casting a half smile in my general direction and then nodding to me as he hurried by without stopping on his way. I continued my tour of the grounds and the woods, enjoying the peace and tranquillity, stopping to admire the local red squirrels and passing several of the Monks who likewise did not communicate in any way, other than to acknowledging my presence with a nod or a reverential bow of the head.

So our first full day was well on its way. It was only 9am and I felt as if I had been up and busy for hours. The Novice Master had arranged a meeting in the common room to commence our training programme. We were to quickly get into the ways of monastic life. Until now, we still felt like visitors, outsiders, as we were still dressed in our normal outdoor clothes. We had all previously sent our full body measurements to the Novice Master before we had arrived in Perth. Today, we were at last, to really look and feel like Redemptorist Monks. There were twelve new Novices including myself at Kinnoull. For us, this was a defining moment. To dress as the other Priests and Monks gave us a genuine feeling of belonging. The clothing we were about to wear would set us apart from other people and let everyone know who we were and what we were all about. The habit consisted of a full length black robe, crossing over the chest from left to right and with a white fastening neck collar held together by a thick six inch belt around the waist. Hanging from the belt was a large and long set of black Rosary Beads. This contained fifteen sets of beads as opposed to the normal set of five on a standard set, as used by Catholics in general. The habit was made of a thick and heavy gabardine type material. At first, it felt really heavy and cumbersome. It was normally worn over trousers and a tea shirt, or similar type of shirt without a collar. Of course, it was soon to become obvious as to why it needed to be so heavy. The monastery was nearly always cold and quite simply, it was meant to keep the wearer warm. However, even the habit was not enough to cope with the cold in winter or when walking outside and there was an outside garment that was worn over the habit. This consisted again of a full length black cloak, with a large hood. As I stood there, along with all the Novices, trying on the new garb, I began already to feel different. I had a feeling of excitement, of expectation, and yes a feeling of belonging. As I glanced around the room at the other Novices in their new clothing, we were all smart young men, a new influx of Novices from a new era. Most of us had arrived with long hair. This was, after all 1966, the age of the Beatles and the Rolling Stones, the swinging sixties and we were youths of our generation. Before the fitting of the habits, we had received the obligatory haircut. This was done by one of the brothers with a barbers cutter and scissors. It was hardly stylish but not quite as severe as the US Army style of haircut. Even so, it was a shock to the system to have our locks shorn so short. It was the equivalent of a crew cut. We were soon to learn though, that vanity of any sort was not to be tolerated. Even so, it was hard not to feel a flush a pride because we looked young, fresh and smart in our new habits. We were an intake of badly needed new blood into the Monastery. A new generation of Novice Monks that would fortify the existing ranks of ageing brothers and clerics. We were in stark contrast to many of the older Brothers. Age and hard work had taken its toll on them, as they had been living and working for many years in the monastery. Their habits had become stained and dirty and rough around the edges and cuffs, due to many years of wear and tear. The colour had become a dirty grey rather than pristine black such as ours. Many of the elder brothers were stooped and walked badly, showing the age and ailments of many years of unselfish service to the Redemptorists and to God. No longer did they care greatly about their appearance. Many rarely left the Monastery grounds, if at all. Without doubt they had higher ideals in their minds than to worry about the state of their dirty habits. The contrast however was decidedly marked. We were a dozen new recruits, at a time when fewer and fewer young men were joining religious orders. At this one moment in time, the new and the old had come together in a common cause, but times were changing fast, and the old monastic ways and habits were about to change forever, but the change was not going to be during this year or anytime very soon.

Our first full day at Perth was about to start in earnest. Here we were, fresh and new and all kitted out in our monastic robes, and we certainly looked the part, but were we ready for the life that it entailed? Only time would tell.

The Novice Master's role was to introduce and to integrate the Novices, into monastic life, and especially into the Redemptorist way of life. We were different from many other orders of Monks and Clerics. Unlike Cistercian Monks and other types of enclosed Orders, we were not entirely a silent community, as the Redemptorists were also a missionary order and our objective was to go out into the community and preach the word. However, silence was certainly a key part of the life, and large periods of each day were to be spent without speaking as preparation for the work that was to be done in the community. We were to live within the rule of our founder, St.Alphonsus de Liguori of Italy. He was the founder member of the Redemptorists and had written a set of rules by which the members of the order were to live. This however was around the year 1730 when life was substantially different and much more severe in so many ways. Yet here we were in 1966, and we were still to live by the same rule and indeed much of the lifestyle was very similar to those days of the eighteenth century.

The Novice Master gathered us together in the common room and explained to us that once we had donned the habit, we also took on a new way of life. However, although we looked like Monks, we were not. We were novices, and we were to spend a full year on trial, to see if the monastic life was the one for us. We were to live the life of a monk in exactly the same way as the elder brothers and priests who had lived here for very many years.

The cornerstones of the Redemptorist monastic life were the three vows that we were planning to take at the end of our year as a novice. These were the vows of poverty, chastity and obedience. The vows were not be taken lightly, and if at the end of the year, I were to commit to them, then they would be fully binding on me, by my own free choice in the eyes of God and the community, if not the law of the land. It was a serious commitment to make.

The vow of poverty meant that, quite literally, I would own nothing at all. Everything I would use would belong to the Redemptorist community, but as a person, as an individual, I would own nothing. The reason for taking a vow of poverty is that I would not be encumbered by the pursuit of money or possessions. These are the very things that would distract from the life I was planning to sign up to. Indeed, it is not difficult to understand the logic behind the thinking, and if I were to have no concerns about money and possessions then I could dedicate all my time and efforts to the life of a monk, a priest and a missionary. Of course, like every institution in life, money had to be earned to live and some possessions were necessary, but these then all belonged to the Redemptorist community. The money required for living this life was received in a number of ways. Donations from the community have always been an important contribution, but the monks would also earn income from the services they offered. These included the giving of missions, retreats, weddings, baptisms, funerals and the like, where the payment for these would help to pay for the upkeep of the monastery and its simplistic life-style. Whatever was earned by the monks or donated to any individual member of the Order would go directly into the communal Redemptorist purse, so that the Monastery could continue its simple lifestyle and provide their religious and social services to the local and national communities.

As a novice, I did not pay for myself and I was unable to contribute anything to the Monastery finances. Other than the clothes I arrived in, I no longer owned anything and I was totally dependant upon the Redemptorists for my keep. However, it was never about money and personal possessions, and as long as we had enough to live on, then we needed no more. The whole idea of the vow of poverty was to concentrate on matters other than money and as such, we did indeed live a very simple and fairly poor existence. The food that we ate was wholesome, and there was enough of it, but it was simple and inexpensive. Much of it was grown in the fields that belonged to the monastery and the type of food we ate was plain and very simple. So too was the clothing and necessary items we needed for the monastery. Nothing was purchased out of the communal purse, unless it was essential and there were very few if any extravagances at all. As if to confirm the point, we had to ask permission from the Novice Master for anything that we may require, even necessary and basic toiletry items such as razor blades. The norm was to keep a razor blade for a month. I tried to use the same Gillette Silver razor blade for as long as possible. After about four weeks the blade was so blunt that it began to hurt and cut me as I dragged it across my face. I went to the Novice Master with some trepidation and asked him if I could have a new razor blade. He went through the process of asking me if I really needed a new razor blade before he eventually agreed to give me a new one, which he went and obtained from the locked store cupboard. This was poverty in action. Although we were not short of any basics and essentials, we were made aware that we were to live as poorly and as simply as possible and that nothing would be provided to us unless there was a genuine and necessary need for it.

The vow of poverty was brought well and truly home to me quite early into my noviciate. I came to Perth on 1st September 1966 and I "celebrated" my 18th birthday on 17th September, just less than three weeks after I had arrived. We were not encouraged to communicate with anybody outside the noviciate during the year that we were novices. We were only permitted to write to our family once a month, and so my birthday was the first communication I had made with them, since I had arrived. On 17th September the Novice Master came to me in my cell and he handed me a letter containing a birthday card and a parcel. I opened the parcel with some anticipation and excitement to find that there was a typewriter inside. I had told my parents that I would really like a typewriter some months earlier. Of course, I knew the rules, and so I took the typewriter to the Novice Master. He asked me to put it on the table in his cell, and I left. Later that night he came to me in the common room at recreation and he said:

"Brother Stephen, it is very kind of your parents to send you a typewriter, but clearly you do not need it, so I have given it to Father Johnston who will find it very useful in his Missionary work. Give our thanks to your parents for

their generous gift. It will be put to very good use"

As he walked away, I felt really crestfallen. I knew that in the rules I would not be permitted any items unless it was necessary for me. But when the time came, I had secretly hoped that the Novice Master would let me keep it. So when he took it away from me and gave it to someone who needed it more than I did, I could not help but feel upset at the decision. This was poverty in action. More than anything, it was the emotional attachment of the gift, as it had been sent to me by my own parents on my special 18th birthday. I think that I was also feeling somewhat homesick at the time which made it worse. I was still trying to get used to the totally new way of life and I felt quite crestfallen. Perhaps the problem was that my 18th birthday had come so soon after joining the noviciate and that it was a complete non-event. I was not sure what to expect, but if I had still been living at home, then I know for sure that my 18th birthday would have been a big occasion. I was certainly going to have to get used to things being very different. I did not tell Mum and Dad that their present had gone to one of the priests. I was not sure how they would take it and would they understand? As it was, my birthday did not go totally uncelebrated. Just when I thought that it was not even going to receive a mention, the Novice Master announced during evening recreation that it was Brother Stephen's 18th.birthday and that I had now come of age. There was even a birthday card presented to me and signed by all the novices. Even more, the Novice Master announced that to celebrate my birthday he was authorising the passing around of a tin of chocolates! Apparently, this was the monastery's method of celebrating special occasions and holy days. It was just as well, because I loved chocolate!

I had certainly learned the hard way about the vow of poverty that we were all planning to undertake at the end of a year. I soon got over the disappointment regarding the typewriter and in the cold light of day it was the right thing to do. I actually had no real need of a typewriter and it had been put to good use with Father Johnston. The truth was that we were living a simple and fairly poor lifestyle, but even so, we had everything in life that we needed, which people in genuine poverty do not. Time would indeed tell, but I believed that I could eventually come to terms with living under with vow of poverty.

The vow of obedience which the Redemptorists took meant that the monks had to live by the rule of St. Alphonsus, and obey all the rules contained in it. This was all documented in detail, and became the rule by which we lived our lives. In addition, all the monks had to obey the rules of their superiors. This meant that every instruction from the smallest of directions to the largest must be obeyed without question and without complaint. For me, and many of the young novices, this was no great hardship. As boys from as early as eleven years of age, we were used to being instructed and controlled by our tutors who were also Redemptorist Priests or Monks. The life at Perth was now a continuation of the Juvenate at Erdington, but now at a much higher level of intensity. The life of unquestioned obedience could be similarly compared to life in any of the armed forces where instructions from any superior are carried out to the letter and without complaint. Just as a soldier can be ordered to go to Afghanistan at a moments notice, a Redemptorist Priest or Monk can be instructed to operate from any monastery or Church in the country and carry out any task or job as required by his superior. He could also be posted abroad to any of the countries where Missions are carried out or where the Redemptorists live and operate.

On a daily basis, the monastic routine was long established and the rule was observed and tasks were carried out as instructed. Obedience in a Redemptorist monastery was a natural occurrence and would not normally be an issue. However, there could of course be instances where an instruction by a superior may have far reaching consequences on the life of a monk or priest and may be against his natural wishes. In these instances, obedience then becomes difficult to observe, but it must be carried out, and the wishes of the individual would take second place to that of the overall wish of the community.

Whereas the vows of obedience and poverty can sometimes be difficult to accept and understand, they can at least come naturally to some extent. However, the vow of Chastity for a man can seem to be the most difficult of all and also against nature and the natural order. The same may be said for women, but I am unable to really comment on that. Many people find it extremely difficult, if not impossible, to understand how a man can take a vow to lead a completely celibate life. In common with all Catholic Priests, the Redemptorist Monks and Brothers all take a lifelong vow of chastity, otherwise known as celibacy. This means living the life of a single man. The sole purpose of this is to have the time to dedicate life to God and to his work, by not having the commitment, distraction and time required by having a wife and family.

As I listened to the Novice Master explaining the vows that we were planning to take, it came across my mind that I would not have any major problem with the vow of poverty and with the vow of obedience. I did quite wonder if and how I would cope in the long-term with the vow of chastity. All throughout my teenage years at the Juvenate, I had spent all my years in the company of boys and men. There was nothing really unusual with that, as private and public school boys are educated in the same way. The difference was that boys at normal boarding school still had regular communication with girls, whereas my upbringing was almost exclusively with boys alone. With the exception of a fleeting time with a girl named Jill at the end of my Juvenate years, I had very little understanding or communication with girls. It was little wonder then, that I was always very shy and bashful when I came into any contact or conversation with them. True, I did have a younger sister, and we were very close, but I saw very little of her, as I lived away from home from the age of eleven, and she also left home early to pursue her career. At this stage, my main concern was whether I could manage to live a solitary life, for although I would be living in a community, the long periods of silence and the lack of any close and personal relationships may be too much to manage without. I was not sure if I would be strong enough to cope with that type of lifestyle.

For the present though, I was not going to worry about

that possibility. Despite my natural reservations and my genuine anxiety about the future, I was actually on a real high. I was feeling motivated, even excited and I was ready to give this new life my very best shot. I had a genuine belief in my religion and I was one hundred per cent convinced in my belief in God and that he had called me to serve him in this extraordinary lifestyle. I felt honoured and in awe, that I was one of the few people that had been called to be a priest. In my mind, I was totally committed to becoming a fully fledged member of the Redemptorists. There was, however still a long way to go to achieve this goal. First and foremost I had to complete my noviciate and be invited to join the order, and then I would have to move onto to Hawkstone, in Shropshire the senior seminary where I would have to spend six years of intensive study in order to qualify to become a priest. At fifteen minutes before 1pm the monastery bell tolled. This told all the Monks, whether they were outside in the fields or inside the monastery grounds or building, to stop whatever they were doing and come inside for lunch. Until the end of this meal, unless there was a special reason, then all work and tasks were carried out in silence. My job was to work on the farm under the direction of Brother Michael in the pig sty. It mainly involved cleaning out the sty and providing food and bedding for the pigs. It was not the most glamorous of jobs, but that was the vow of obedience! I did whatever was asked of me, I had to do it, and do it with a smile and without complaint. After all, this was to provide food and help to pay for the running of the monastery. Even so, coming from a town lifestyle in Manchester, it was hard to get used to country ways and to accept that we were rearing pigs on the farm and then eating them for our own food.

As I heard the bell toll, I quickly dropped what I was doing and headed back towards my cell to clean myself up in readiness for lunch. We all gathered together once more to eat a meal. Again, the food was simple but wholesome and much of the food was as a result of the work we had been doing on the farm. We had to be as self sufficient as we were able. I had never eaten so healthily; fresh fruit and vegetables from the farm and orchard, with either meat or fish and simply cooked and presented. The meal was a main course followed by a simple dessert usually involving a cake and custard or rice. As always the meal was eaten without any conversation. It was not the done thing to ask for the salt or pepper to be passed to you. It was up-to each individual to ensure that each brother had what was required. Then one of the brothers would say grace and then proceed to the pulpit to read out loud for the benefit of the others. At lunch-time, the reading was usually a religious biography. I had never been a great reader so it was at least a passive way of reading without actually having to make the effort to do it myself.

After we had taken lunch, it was tradition to take a short walk around the garden. We were never encouraged to make particular friendships with any individual as we were expected to have the same relationship with everyone in the community, so after lunch we had to mix with whichever monk happened to be the nearest as we left the refectory. My natural inclination was to seek the company of the young novices that we had come with, some of which were my friends, but more often that not I ended up walking with one of the older monks for our lunch-time constitutional. It was a fifteen minute stroll around the grounds and after lunch until evening time, we were permitted to speak. I had always been of a shy and reserved nature, so I did not find it easy to speak with the older monks. After spending so much time in silence, it would be natural to want to talk whenever there was an opportunity, but the truth was, I was in awe of the older monks. They seemed to be so wise and experienced about life and seemed to be so calm and content with the hard life they had chosen. I was just fascinated to listen to them. After all, I was just an eighteen year old novice with very limited experience of life. Despite leading what appeared to be a very small and enclosed life, the older monks had such an amazing wealth of stories and experiences, and I was amazed and fascinated to listen to them and I was inspired and encouraged by their wisdom.

In the afternoons, we would return to our work on the farm. For the first month I was allocated to work in the pig sty with Brother Michael. As a boy from the town, this was my first real experience of rural life. It was very different to anything I had experienced. Brother Michael was a giant of a man. He came originally from the south west of Ireland. The Catholic Church in England was largely made up of priests, brothers, nuns and monks who came from the very Catholic country of Ireland. It was synonymous with religious people from Ireland who had come to live and practice in the British Isles. Brother Michael was a no nonsense type of man, totally different to the person you would expect to be a religious Brother. He was loud, brash even abrasive, but extremely kind and he had dedicated himself to this simple life on the farm and in the monastery. He looked anything but a religious man. He looked just like a farmer in a religious habit, and a dirty habit it was too. He didn't care about how he looked, sounded or dealt with people. He just got on with his work and did his own thing, but he was totally committed to the religious life and very happy with it. To say that I was in awe of this man was a big understatement and I was very soon to look up to him as a role model.

One day he asked me to muck out the pig sties. There were more than twenty pigs on the farm, so there was a lot of mucking out to do. I was shovelling muck from the sty into a wheelbarrow and moving it to the gardens. As I was doing this, I was on a narrow path and the wheelbarrow started to slide down the side of the path and down a hill. I tried to rectify the wheelbarrow and attempted to twist the handles to keep it on the path, but in doing so I lost control of the barrow which went down the hill and in the process I twisted my back and injured myself. I was in extreme pain and could barely walk. Brother Michael came to help me and a doctor was called. I was confined to the monastery's infirmary and I was there as a patient for over two weeks of bed rest as I slowly recovered.

The time in the infirmary was very frustrating and the days just seemed to drag on and be longer and longer. I had been told by the local doctor to lie flat on my back and do very little. I most certainly had time to think as I spent most of the time doing little else. I did of course have visitors, but in keeping with the silence and the general life-style, these were few and far between. My most frequent visitor was Brother Michael who came to see me at least every day. He would bring me some reading material, mostly religious books or magazines, so when he suggested something else a little lighter, I was only too pleased. We had chatted about all sorts of things, and he knew that one of my biggest passions in life before coming to Perth was football and Manchester City in particular. Since I had been at Perth, with no radio, television or newspapers, I was completely unaware of what was happening in the outside world and to my beloved Manchester City. I had told Brother Michael that at home I used to read the Manchester Evening News Football Pink every week. He said: *"Why don't you write to your Mother and ask her to post it to me and I will get it across to you?"* He probably knew that as a novice I was not allowed such literature and that any post that was sent to novices was opened and inspected by the novice master. I was somewhat surprised that he made this offer. I knew that I was not allowed to receive any newspapers from outside. He could see that I was nervous of agreeing to this but he said: *"Oh go on! I'll not tell anyone! Get your Mammy to send it to me every week, and I'll bring it to you."* I was shocked and surprised, but also very pleased. Between us, we had planned this deceit and broken the rules, and yet because it had been suggested by Brother Michael who I respected greatly, I somehow managed to convince myself that it was alright and that it was just a minor breach of the rules. And so, I arranged it with my Mother who posted the football pink to me every week from then on. On the last week that I was in the infirmary, Brother Michael brought the football paper to me. Of course, I read it in secret and hid it under my pillow when anyone came into the infirmary to visit me. It was just great to know what was going on the world of sport as I missed my football very much. And I had been very bored during my two weeks in the infirmary.

When I had recovered I went back to my normal duties assisting Brother Michael on the pig farm, albeit I was on lighter duties for quite some time. There was a boot room inside the monastery, where we would leave our normal shoes and change into working footwear. Brother Michael had arranged with me to place my "Football Pink" newspaper into my Wellington Boots when it arrived each week by post. We did this for several weeks and I would collect it from one of my "wellies" where he had hidden it and then slip it under my habit before taking it to my cell to read. Although I did this for a number of weeks, I never felt entirely comfortable with it, knowing that it was a deceit, and that it was against all the rules. However, I managed to convince myself that it was alright to carry on doing it and treated it as only a very minor fault.

Some weeks later, as I was preparing to go outside to work, the Novice Master came into the boot room. He came straight up to me and handed me a package. I knew exactly what it was. It was my football pink. It was still unopened with a brown paper wrapper covering much of the paper, but it was clear to see what it was. It was addressed to Brother Michael at The Monastery address. As he handed the paper to me, he just said in a very quietly spoken voice: *"Is this for you, Brother Nearey?"* I took it from him. *"Yes father:"* I replied, in an even lower and nervous voice. Nothing else was said: I could see the disappointment in his eyes and hear it in his voice. As he handed the "contraband" to me unopened, he turned swiftly on his heels and marched away to leave me to deal with my own thoughts and my guilty conscience.

I was mortified: I went straight back to my cell and took the offending paper with me. I put it onto my table, leaving it un-opened, and going over and over in my mind, the magnitude of what I had done. The fact that the Novice Master had said nothing to me, made it much, much worse. I knew that he was leaving it up-to me to do the right thing. The next afternoon, we gathered as always in the common room, just the Novices and the Novice Master. It was a regular session based on honesty. We all had to be totally honest with ourselves and our brothers, and we had to live not only by the law of the Ten Commandments, but also the rule of St. Alphonsus the founder of the Redemptorists. The rule covered all details of the life we were living in the monastery. We sat around in a circle making rosary beads which was something that we did everyday. I suppose you could call it a cottage industry possibly even a therapy. Then in keeping with the Catholic tradition of confession, each of the Novices would have to confess out loud to the others, any faults or rules that they had broken since the previous confession, usually each day. As could be expected, the type of faults and breaking of the rules were matters such as talking during periods of silence, unkind thoughts or actions, failing to carry out an instruction of one's superior. In fact, there were so many laws and practices within the rules of the order that it was almost impossible not to have a long list of things to confess every day. Each imperfection needed to be eradicated in the search and drive for perfection, which was the objective of the Order. These faults would hardly be serious and impeachable crimes in the outside world, but in the religious life that we were living; each and everyone would feel serious and needed to be confessed to our brothers and eradicated.

As the Novice Master went around the room asking each Novice to confess their faults, there was the usual mix of minor demeanours, occasionally there were more serious ones, and each Novice confessing their faults had to beg the forgiveness of the Novice Master and The Brothers, and these would be punished by a penance handed out by the Novice Master. This would normally be a punishment of additional prayers, for example, saying an extra round of the Rosary, or the Lords Prayer twenty times over.

When it was my turn, the Novice Master looked at me, he said: *"Brother Nearey, have you anything to confess?"* *"Yes Father"*, I said, very quietly, and feeling extremely sheepish and humbled in front of my colleagues and Brothers. *"I have broken the rule of obedience by bringing reading material into the monastery without permission and with the intention of deceiving you. Not only this, but I have done this for several weeks, and continued this deceit, and at the same time have failed to confess this to you and my brothers on many, many occasions."* The room fell silent. I imagine that the other Novices were quite shocked, although I never discussed it with any of them. I felt that the whole room was looking at me. Whatever was revealed in these confessions was never spoken about again outside of the Novice sessions.

The Novice Master looked me directly in the eye and said: *"Are you sorry for these demeanours Brother?"* I replied that I was extremely sorry, not only for getting caught out, but for deceiving my fellow Novices and the Novice Master, in defiance of the rules. In all truth, I was extremely sorry and felt mortified. To me, and perhaps the others, this was a serious breaking of the rule of obedience and a deceit, when our life was supposed to be all about complete honesty. My punishments were several: First of all, I had to apologise to my fellow Novices for breaking their trust. Secondly, I had to ask forgiveness of the Novice Master, and to apologise to Brother Michael for putting him in a position of aiding and abetting my disobedience. No doubt Brother Michael too, would have to confess likewise to his own Superior, for assisting me in this deceit. Finally, I was given the additional job of cleaning out the boot room [the scene of the crime], every day for the next four weeks.

I thought that this was the end of my world! It may have seemed trivial but it was not. I also felt the need to confess this matter in the confessional, to another Priest. That was the only way, finally that I felt completely forgiven and able to move on again and strive to become the Monk that I, as a Novice was striving to become.

Monastery life was one of routine after routine. Days were very much like each other with repetition being the same theme. Each day was based on lengthy periods of prayer, silence, reading, work, association, meditation and more silence, interspersed with meal breaks! Nearly all the time was spent within the monastery walls, but there were periods when we were able to go outside and mingle with the outside world. Looking out from the windows of the monastery could also feel prison like. We could see the outside world, but not really take part in it. Unlike the fully fledged Monks and Priests, we had no good reason to mingle with the local community. Many was the time during the long autumn days and evenings, when I would look out from my cell on the top story, and see the twinkling lights of the town in Perth and wonder just what was going on out there, and with a touch of envy, that I was unable to explore the local town and all that it had to offer. There were other trips out from the monastery, albeit few and far between. The whole idea of the Noviciate was to establish if I and the Novices were cut out for this unusual lifestyle, so most of our time in Perth was spent inside the monastery and living the quiet contemplative life. Each day though, in the afternoon, there would be a period of free association. This usually meant that we walked and talked in the gardens with the other Novices or Monks, or if the weather was inclement, which was often the case in Scotland, then the time would be spent in the Common room making rosary beads, or playing draughts or quietly reading. From a young age, I had always hated being enclosed and I had a fear of confined spaces. This was in later life to turn into a great fear of lifts and being confined anywhere at all. I developed a feeling of claustrophobia which would stay with me for life. As a result of this, I always felt the need to be outside in the open as much as possible, and if I was inside, then I felt hemmed in, if I was in a small room and I always sought out large open spaces, even indoors. Very often in the monastery, I yearned to be outside, and I worried a lot about being indoors for so much of the time. During periods of free association, we were permitted on certain days to spend these outside, so I would jump at the chance to walk outside of the monastery confines and stroll in the large open spaces. Usually this would be with the other novices, but there were days when the weather was bad and nobody wanted to walk outside. But for me being outside gave me a sense of freedom. I felt liberated once I was in open spaces and my mood lightened. This was even more so once I was outside the monastery confines. This was perhaps not a good omen for things to come. Occasionally, when the weather was bad, I would walk alone up to the top of Kinnoull Hill, a few hundred yards from the Monastery, from where there was a panoramic view of the Tay Valley. The river Tay could be seen meandering its way through the lush green landscape. From the top of the hill, there were dramatic views of the rolling mountains unfolding in front of my eyes. One could see hunting lodges and forests for miles around. Here I felt a strange sense of quiet and peace. Strangely, although I was hundreds of miles from my real home, I felt a real sense of inner peace that I did not feel inside the Monastery. It did concern me that I felt this need for escapism and I wondered if I would ever really be settled and content. It was unusual to seek out time walking on my own as I spent so much time in silence inside the Monastery walls, but I had to offset this against a nervous feeling of confinement and being enclosed, as I spent so much of my time inside the monastery enclosure.

The days passed by and weeks turned into months. The daily routine and rituals became the norm and I became more and more engrossed in the monastic lifestyle. On the one hand I had very genuine worries and concerns that I could never settle to the monastic life, but on the other hand there were times when I felt totally engrossed in it and happy about the future and genuinely excited about the prospect of my life as a Monk and a missionary Priest.

Perhaps one of the biggest problem areas facing me was to be the management of my personal relationships. The Novices were always encouraged to be all things to all men. By that, it meant that a monk was to encourage the same type of relationship with all the other monks and that no personal relationship should mean more than another. Close individual friendships were not meant to happen at Perth and were frowned upon. I found this particularly difficult as I had always chosen close friends in the Juvenate at Erdington. I used to spend time with my friends. This seemed completely normal and the others were the same, with most of the lads having their own friends to spend time with, but now it all had to change.

It did not help however, when two of my Juvenate friends who had come to Perth at the same time as I had, decided to leave and go back home. It happened one day early in November. The Novice Master got up to speak at breakfast time. This in itself was unusual as we rarely ever spoke before lunchtime. He just addressed us while we were eating and said that Brother Declan had decided that he wanted to return to his home and that the monastic life was not for him. This announcement came like a lightening bolt out of the blue. To all appearances, Declan had seemed to have settled to the life and I had no reason to suspect that he would not continue. I had not known him before he arrived at Perth, but I had grown to like him although he had not been somebody that I classed as a close friend. His departure came as a blow to my own confidence. Of all the Novices at Perth, he was perhaps one of the men I had expected to go all the way. He certainly gave the impression that he was quiet, studious and that he was happy with the life. For several days later, I felt rather down and worried. I wondered what had happened for him to take the decision to leave. I had not known him long but I saw him as a strong and determined character and I definitely expected him to go on and take his vows and continue on to become a priest. The Novice Master just asked us to pray for him that he would settle into the normal life of a lay-person back home with his family, but there was never an explanation as to his reasons for returning home. Over the coming days the Novice Master spoke to us and explained in general terms that the Monastic life was not for everyone. It was only for those people that had received the calling and had been chosen. He explained that we do not initially choose a life of being a Monk or a Priest. The calling is from God and that he chooses us. It is for us to either accept or reject that calling. In some ways, this explanation somewhat pacified me. I began to understand that Declan had not been called and that he had realised this and returned back home.

I was just beginning to settle back down and return to the normal routine when I had another massive shock. One of my friends, John who had been with me at the Juvenate, came to my cell one evening. I had just settled down to do some reading when there was a very quiet tapping on my cell door. It was not the done thing to go to one another's cells and of course it broke the evening curfew which was one of strict silence. As I reacted to the tapping on my cell door, I expected to see the Novice Master stood there. Instead, there was my friend. He looked sheepish, and in a very quietly spoken voice, barely a whisper, he asked me if he could come in. I glanced around the cloister and all was quiet. It was dark and there was nobody around. It was against the rules to speak, of course, but even so, I could see that all was not right and I beckoned him to come in. He had been at the Juvenate with me for six years, and we had grown up together, we knew each other well, and yes, I did regard him as a friend. He came in and sat down at the end of my bed. He could barely let the words come out of his mouth, and he did not want to be heard. The walls seemed very thin and there were cells on either side of me. In the silence of the monastery, almost any noise would be noticed. So he whispered very quietly: *"Steve, I'm sorry, but I am leaving in the morning".* He was apologetic and very nervous as he spoke. It was almost as if he was confessing to a murder or some equally deadly deed. He could see the shock on my face. I said nothing for quite some time. After what seemed a very long silence, I just whispered: *"Why".* I did not know what else to say. He hesitated, thought about it for some time and then replied in a low whisper: *"I just can't see myself doing this for the rest of my life!"* I knew exactly what he meant. That same thought had crossed my mind on so many occasions. Immediately, I wondered why I had not been brave enough to come to the same conclusion. In an instant, I felt envious that it was not me that that taken that decision. He left and returned to his cell for one last night at Perth, and tomorrow he was gone. The following morning, John did not attend meditation, and he was not at Mass or at breakfast. The Novice Master announced that he had left the Monastery for good to return to civil life and that his family had collected him early that morning. I was not of course surprised, but from the shock on the other Novices' faces, I was the only one that had known in advance. Whereas that night I had been in shock and wished that I too had left, by the next morning I felt totally different. I could not understand quite why, but I felt proud of who I was. I felt proud of what I was doing and what I was going to be. To be dressed as a Monk, and living in a Monastery, gave to me a form of status that I was proud to have. As a Monk, humility was always a trait that we were supposed to aspire to. Status was not something that we were trying to achieve. I had always had low self esteem since being a young boy and my lack of self confidence had always been a feature of my personality. To become a Novice Monk with all that it entailed, gave me a major goal in life that I could strive for, and for the first time ever, I began to feel that I was somebody that people could respect. The position of Priest and Monk were positions that held respect, and even if they were not the roles that other people would aspire to it was now my life's ambition.

I had just lost two of my friends and fellow novices in a short space of time, yet despite this loss, it seemed to galvanise me into trying even harder to become what they could not. In an unusual way, my friend's decision to leave made me more determined to succeed if I possibly could, and I was more than ever determined to stay put.

As the autumn days turned into winter, I felt that I had been in the Noviciate in Perth for years, yet I had been living there for just a few short months. The regular routine, the long periods of silence, and the enclosed lifestyle all conspired to make the time pass very slowly. The only changes to the strict regime were the regular feast days of the Saints which were celebrated. Whereas the outside world would keep their bank holidays, we celebrated the main days of the Christian Calendar. The Saint's days were remembered in our own style. Normal routine was suspended, and there were longer periods of recreation. Instead of readings at meal times and silence, we had free association with our colleagues and silence was replaced with talking. Even the food was different. Instead of simple and plain fare, special meals were provided on Saints days and particularly at Christmas and Easter, the main holidays of the year. At recreation times, sweets and chocolates were given out and the strict rules of silence were cancelled for that feast-day. Periods of normality though were replaced by other unusual and outdated types of behaviour, more fitting to the middle ages than to the 20th.Century. In the outside world, even the Catholic Church, which is known for its strict procedures and laws, was very slowly coming to terms with the modern age. The post war years of austerity had given way to a brand new modern age outside, known as the Swinging Sixties. Freedom and Peace were the new watch-words But in monastic life, time moved on very slowly, and rules, traditions and ways of life changed ever so slowly, if at all. The fact that Monastic Life was so austere and cut off from the outside world, meant that traditions stayed much the same and change was desperately slow and reluctant. In 1966, Latin was still the official language of the Catholic Church, although The Church of England had changed to the English language decades before. Mass in the Catholic Church was celebrated completely in Latin, as were other services. Most people attending those services would have learned the Latin language in Church, in "parrot fashion". But most would not know what they were actually saying when they prayed and chanted in the Latin language. This was typical of the slowness and reluctance to change that was still greatly in evidence and was holding back the Church from becoming more relevant to the modern era.

Some of the traditions in the Monastery were much slower to change and would be viewed as quite shocking in this modern day and age. One of the old traditions going back hundreds of years was that of self-chastisement. In the days of St. Alphonsus who founded the Redemptorists and wrote the rule by which the members lived their lives, the pursuit of perfection was so strong that monks would punish themselves if they failed to live their lives strictly according to the rule. Many of the Monks would inflict pain on themselves if they failed to live up-to their own high ideals and objectives. The wearing of a "hair-shirt" was common-place in 1732 when the order was founded.

A hair shirt is a coarse garment which was intended to be worn next to the skin, thus keeping the wearer in a state of discomfort and constant awareness of the shirt's presence. Such garments were traditionally worn by some members of Christian religious orders, along with individuals who felt penitent about certain actions of their lifestyles. The use of hair shirts is fairly limited in the modern era, but the term is often used metaphorically, which is why someone might refer to wearing a "hair shirt" when they perform some other act of self-imposed penitence. Even more extreme and medieval was the use of a leather whip with several tails containing sharp ends. Monks in many religious orders would chastise themselves for the smallest of imperfections in their own life. Here we are talking about what the outside world would view as very minor imperfections. Perhaps a monk would have had an unkind thought about another person, or failed to carry out an instruction of a superior and although he would almost certainly confess this to a priest in the confessional, he may also choose to punish himself by the use of this type of whip, which he would keep in his cell. At times like this he would lash his own back causing significant pain and even bleeding. I was shocked to find out that while I was a Novice at Perth, that some of the older Monks were still practicing this form of self punishment. It could even be heard in adjoining cells or whilst walking along the silent cloisters. Personally, I found this practice to be very old fashioned and extremely distasteful, but some of the older Monks had been brought up in this strict code of practice. They began their monastic lives in a far more austere age, so it was not fair to apply the latest and more modern thinking to the new monastic life-style. I felt pleased that the new batch of Novices were far more outward looking and focused on the missionary aspect of the order, whilst the older monks were just the opposite, and were inward looking and focused more on themselves and the contemplative aspect of their life. "Old habits die hard", as the expression goes, and while the older Monks lived their lives in the manner which they had been accustomed to, it was essential for the future of the Redemptorists that change would take place in the near future. Already, it was becoming more difficult to attract young men to the Order and despite the influx of twelve new Novices that year, the fall-out rate was far too high and there were less and less new vocations each year to replace the older members of Monks who had died off.

In the 1960's we witnessed a substantial period of change. The country had experienced two World Wars, the second of which had finished only some fifteen years earlier. The country was still recovering both financially and socially and attitudes particularly with young people were changing quickly. The new generation no longer followed their parents into the same jobs that they had. Transport was improving and people could move around much more easily and take other kinds of work in far off places. Attitudes were also changing both in society and in religion. Youngsters were deciding for themselves if they wanted to believe what they and their parents had been taught. No longer would they blindly accept the Christian teaching. Like wise, the Church was experiencing similar reactions. Attendances at church services were down and becoming few and fewer. Congregations were becoming older as fewer people attended church services. Likewise, the new generation were not being attracted to a Church which was still hundreds of years behind the times and the numbers joining the priesthood and going into Monasteries was becoming worryingly small. The Popes and the Catholic teachings were still extremely conservative in their attitudes and they were no longer connecting with the people in the way that they had in years gone by. Likewise, the Redemptorist Order was mirroring the happenings in the Catholic Church at large. Monastic Orders such as ours were perhaps even more outdated than the Church in the wider communities and parishes. The very nature of enclosed Monasteries meant that traditions were maintained for much longer and change, if any, was going to be desperately slow.

In the Redemptorist Order, our generation of Novices and newly ordained Priests were perhaps the first to start questioning the old order of things and the ways and traditions of the past. However, this was done discreetly and in such a way as not to question the wisdom and authority of our elders and superiors. Despite the fact that we too had been brought up in a very traditional manner, we were then young people of a new age, the "Swinging Sixties", with its new music, and new attitudes to everything in life, and with the new world technology about to explode into our society, it really did feel like a new way of life was about to dawn. However, this was for sometime in the near future and with the existing older members still at the helm, change was not going to happen very quickly, but change it must if the Order was to survive and thrive in the decades to come.

Fourteen

Decision Time

On the one hand, time moved interminably slow in the Noviciate, and the days seemed to meander leisurely from one day to another, in a very carefree and unhurried manner, and yet from a different perspective, a year had never flown by as quickly as it now seemed to have done. Perhaps it was that I had reached yet another milestone. Maybe it was the necessity to make a momentous decision very shortly. I had celebrated my "coming of age", my 18th birthday, just a couple of weeks after joining the Noviciate only the previous year. Officially, I was all grown up, able to vote, able to join the army, able to drink in a public house, able to be married, and yet in my own mind, I was still immature, very young and oh so very indecisive. I was more than able to make decisions on many things, able to decide on small and large issues, yet on this one big issue, I seemed powerless to decide. Perhaps there was too much at stake to go one way or the other, and until I really had to do so, I kept my options open and just carried on living the life as best as I could.

September was again approaching; the trees were losing their foliage in the autumn winds and my year as a Novice was shortly coming to an end. The winds of change were indeed blowing through and I knew that for me, I had to decide my future. The past twelve months had been a period of change, of learning, of adapting to a new and different life style. The year of being a Postulant and then a Novice was ending and a date had been set for the formal transition to becoming a Monk and then formally being accepted into the Redemptorist Religious Order.

Although I have many times referred to a decision time, this was now the sole issue on my mind, and that of the other Novices. To the Novice Master and the members of the order, it was not regarded as a "D" Day, merely as a time to formally decide. It was just assumed by them, that we would move on to the next step. The plan was for a seamless transition from Novice to religious Monk. There had been no discussion about the "ifs" and "maybes", and all the assumptions and planning, were that we would all now move onto the next part of our structured journey.

Plans had already been put into operation for the transition. This was meant to be a very big day in our lives. It was akin to a young person in the outside world becoming married. It was a big step, a big deal, and there was a formal day and ceremony to be arranged. The date had been set for 1st.September 1967. Letters had been sent out to members of our families who would attend the ceremony, as they would do a wedding. This day was to be the official acceptance of the Novices into the Redemptorist Order of Monks and the official start of my six year journey to becoming a Missionary and a Priest.

As the summer months began to cool and the leaves began to fall, there was a chill feeling of change in the atmosphere. It was almost September, and it was practically a year since I had arrived at the Monastery in Perth, with some apprehension. Since those early tentative days, I had settled into the monastic way of life and it had become the norm, although it had to be said, that it was a form of institutionalisation in an extreme manner. It seemed an absolute age since I had lived a normal life with my parents and family and I did find it difficult to deal with. There were times when I felt content, and there were other times when I pined to be back with my family and to lead a normal way of life. But now, the date had been set, and my parents and family were making plans to come to Perth and attend the ceremony which would see me take my vows of Poverty, Chastity and Obedience.

Nobody had actually asked me if this was what I was going to do, if this was what I wanted to do, but it was assumed that this was what was going to happen. If I did not want to go through with this, then the only way that it would not happen, would be that I approached the Novice Master and told him that I did not want to become a Religious Monk, and that I wanted to leave and go back to a lifestyle that I had not known since I was eleven years old. If I were to do this, at this very late stage, I would be disappointing not only my parents and family, my friends, but also the many people who had been involved in my upbringing since my early days in Erdington, some eight years earlier. In my mind, I would be disappointing my parents who had paid to send me to the junior seminary at Erdington. I would also be disappointing my tutors and friends who had been with me on this journey for so many years. How on earth could I change my mind and go back to a lifestyle I had not known as an adult. What would people say about me? What would I do in the world outside? I was not trained for anything other than the life I was now living. Yet, I did actually want to become a member of the Redemptorists. I wanted to be a missionary and a monk and really, really believed in God and that he had called me, that he had actually chosen me to join this order and to be a Monk and a Priest. The truth was that I was fearful of the life I was going into. I was afraid of the lonely life. I was living in a Monastery with many other people, but I was still very much alone. I was afraid that I was not good enough to do the job properly, that I was not strong enough and clever enough to see it through.

The days were running out. Doing nothing meant that I was going to continue in the Order and take the next giant step along the pathway. Suddenly, it was indeed, all too late. All the days had run out. I had done nothing to stop the process and therefore I had implicitly agreed to take my vows and to formally join the Redemptorist Order.

1st.September dawned. I awoke in my top floor attic cell with a feeling of apprehension and excitement. I would shortly be seeing my Mum and Dad and my brothers and sister for the first time in a year. I was so looking forward to seeing them again, albeit for a very short time. It would be just one day, and then I would not see them again for at least another year. My elder brother, Arthur, had already made his own momentous step, by becoming a Parish Priest. This gave me all the more drive and motivation to go through with my own vows and head towards the priesthood myself. As I sat in the refectory having my morning breakfast, I was looking forward to seeing them all. It helped to me put my lingering doubts to one side for the moment and to concentrate on seeing my family.

At 11am, I along with ten other Novices walked into the Church for the ceremony. I was heartened by the fact that ten of my colleagues and friends had also decided to take their vows and to formally join the Order alongside me. Perhaps I was worrying unduly? Were any of the other Novices racked with indecision, as I was? If they were, then they did not show it. There were about five of the Novices who had joined with me, aged 11 in 1960, at the Juvenate at Erdington. They were alongside me in the Church, and ready too, to take their vows. It helped me enormously, and just seeing my family in the pews at the front of the Church gave me a massive lift and at that moment, at least momentarily, all my doubts seemed to lift and go away, and at that moment in time, I was ready to dedicate my life to the Redemptorists and to God.

The service was solemn, and full of meaning. In just a few seconds I had committed to make vows to God and to the Redemptorist Order. I had just taken vows of Poverty, Chastity and Obedience. My commitment had been voluntary, and of my own free will, although to say that it was a certainty that I would go ahead, is far from accurate. My decision had been largely a passive one, rather than a definite commitment. I had allowed it to happen, despite much torment and soul-searching. My vow of Poverty was perhaps the least difficult to commit myself to. Perhaps the description of "Poverty" was somewhat wide of the mark, in that most people would apply a different interpretation to it. Real poverty relates to people in third world countries who barely have enough to eat, let alone possessions. The Poverty that I had just vowed to keep was to mean a very different lifestyle to that of truly poor people. In the Monastery we would live very frugally, and in reality I would own nothing for myself and have no money of my own. Even so, everything I would have, and have the use of, would be owned by the Order and not by the individual. However, neither did I want for anything. Food, clothing and all the necessities of life, including a few occasional luxuries, were always provided for by the Redemptorist Order. This had been the case all throughout my years at Erdington, although my parents did pay some tuition fees towards the total costs. At Perth though, I was living completely at the cost of the order and as a Novice was unable to contribute anything at all in terms of finances. This would be the same at Hawkstone and it would not be until I became a Priest, in some six or seven year's time, that I would contribute in financial terms to the upkeep of the Order.

Perhaps the most difficult of all our three vows was the vow of Chastity. In addition to being pure in body and mind, Chastity also meant dedicating one's life entirely to God and this meant that all other relationships had to be secondary. Close relationships of any kind were not encouraged. We were to treat everyone in the same way and no special friendships were permitted. The monastic life excluded marriage to a woman, for all members of the Order, Priests, Brothers and Monks alike. Of all the three vows, this was always going to be the most difficult to cope with in the years to come. The third of the vows was that of obedience. This meant obeying the Rule of the Order in general and specifically obeying the order of a superior. As a boy, obedience to parents and teachers was the norm. Obedience in normal life is a matter of fact. It is compulsory in so many walks of life. The armed forces are very similar, where one has to always obey without questioning the reason why. In employment of all kinds, obedience and following of orders are a pre-requisite of the job. This was to be the same for us but it extended to every aspect of our life and not just while at work. I would need to be forever obedient to my superiors, and to do whatever in life I was asked to do, whether it was a major instruction affecting my life, where I would be stationed, or what I would be doing, or indeed a minor instruction to do something relatively trivial on a daily basis.

The ceremony was then concluded. My vows had been made, and I had committed myself for life to my new and extended family. My own birth family were there to witness it and the families and friends of each of the Novices got together to spend the rest of the day with each other, before we started moving on to the next step on the long and winding road to the Priesthood and becoming a Missionary of the Redemptorist Order.

It felt so good to have my family with me once more. As close as we became to our colleagues in the Redemptorist Order, they could never really take the place of our own families. After the ceremony to take our vows, I spent the remainder of the day with Mum, Dad and the family. It seemed unusual to have them in the Monastery with me as I showed them around. It was a little like an open day and they came to my cell. I think they were slightly shocked at the basic and stark living conditions we had. The public rooms were quite presentable but they seemed really surprised at the tiny attic cell that I had called home for over a year and the living conditions we had accepted. For that one afternoon though, the whole of the Monastery was very different. It was alive and vibrant, and there was a buzz in the air with people walking everywhere. The gardens were full of families strolling around with the Novices and admiring the Monastery building and the beautiful gardens and farm area. Very shortly though, it would return to its quiet self as twelve of the Novices would be moving onto the Seminary at Hawkstone Hall.

Come 6pm, it was all change. The Novice's families either started to leave for home or to go back to the accommodation they were staying in. Normality reigned once more. Quiet had descended on the Monastery and normal service was resumed. It had been a big day and after meditation, supper and recreation, it was time to relax and then retire to bed. I returned to my cell, and as I lay there I pondered the happenings of the day. Tomorrow was to be yet another brand new chapter in my topsy turvy young life. It was the exciting new move to Hawkstone Hall and the third major stop on my demanding and difficult route to the Priesthood after my years spent at Erdington and then Perth.

Fifteen

Moving On

Monday 2nd September dawned. It was a crisp dry day and as the sun rose above the mist on the River Tay, there was a distinctly autumnal feeling in the air. It was a start to the change of the season in Scotland. It was just as if the change from summer to autumn was signalling a significant change for me too. I was about to leave and move to a new and challenging chapter in my own life.

This day somehow felt much different. I was no longer a Novice. I was indeed all grown up and a fully fledged member of the Redemptorists. The usual daily routine was gone though. I awoke and realised that my parents were still there in Perth. They, along with my brothers and sister had stayed at the aptly named Isle of Skye hotel at the bottom of Kinnoull Hill, and after a hearty Scottish breakfast, for them, not for me, they came back to the Monastery to say yet another long goodbye to me. I had not seen any of them for a year, and now after barely one solitary day, I would see them again fleetingly and then bid our fond farewells once more, not knowing when we would see each other again. It was as if I did not belong to them anymore, I now belonged to the Redemptorist family first and foremost. But this was the path I had chosen. It was my own decision, freely made, albeit with some lack of genuine conviction. I now belonged to a new, bigger family, and my own birth family became almost an earlier family of my past. Rightly or wrongly, that is how it felt to me. We chatted about nothing very meaningful in the guest lounge, discussing trivia, and passing more pleasantries before we said our goodbyes. We all seemed a little tense. They then departed in their cars for the long journey south of the border. Again, as with one year before, I felt the pangs of loss as I saw their cars drive out of the entrance and onto the road and away from Perth. It was with a heavy heart that I waved them on their way. My own long journey south was to start very soon after, as all the ex-Novices, now new Redemptorists, would board the coach that would take us all to Hawkstone Hall.

Just a couple of hours later, my suitcase was packed and placed in the entrance hall waiting for our departure. It crossed my mind momentarily that my vow of poverty was very much to the fore. Here I was, moving on to another important chapter of my life, and my total possessions amounted to my monk's habit, and a small number of clothes and personal items such as a toothbrush and a couple of books. Technically, even these did not belong to me, as they belonged to the Order. It was just a fleeting thought, but it reminded me of my new status in life and completely different to life outside the Monastery.

As I was musing, my mind was distracted by my fellow Monks who had all joined me in the entrance, [or should I say "exit" hall. The coach pulled up at the front of the Monastery steps, and several of the "Brothers" loaded our suitcases into the boot. Again, it became a time for more fond farewells. I was about to say goodbye to members of my new extended family. For a full year, I had lived and breathed my life entirely in their company. We had spent every day, twenty fours hours each day, living alongside one another. Despite the fact that just twelve months before, we had been strangers; we had developed a close bond together. Clearly, some relationships were stronger than others. Perhaps the main relationship was with my Novice Master who had controlled and shaped my life over the past year. Yet I had made many strong bonds with the Brothers, Priests, Monks and other Novices. It gave me some confidence and strength that nine of the Novices, who were with me at Perth, were accompanying me on the coach to Hawksone. Even so, it was a wrench to leave the Monastery at Perth. As austere as it had been, and daunting as the past year had been, it had still been home and I had a strange bond and familiarity with it.

As the coach pulled out of the driveway for the long journey south, I turned around and watched the Monastery's imposing structure until it disappeared out of sight as we drove down Kinnoull Hill and headed towards the town of Perth. As its pointed turrets went out of view, I wondered if I would ever return to the Monastery again. At first, I sat quietly in my seat, not engaging in conversation for a while, but deep in my own thoughts and pondering the place that I had called home, and the people I had left behind. I was perhaps seeking some reassurance and consolation. I watched the beautiful green scenery rolling by out of the coach window and then involved myself in conversation with my fellow Monks. At least I was not alone. Three or four of the coach passengers had been with me through six long years since I was an eleven year old boy at the Erdington Juvenate. Other than the school holidays, we had spent every day together from morning until night. We knew each other so well and we had been through so much together. We were on the same journey and I wondered if they had similar feelings to mine. Strangely we hardly ever discussed our inner thoughts, our hopes, wishes, fears and concerns. Whilst at Erdington we had been the best of buddies, we had shared our every thought with the open-ness of youth. Yet, I was barely nineteen years old now and we had all become like recluses, and we had all become older and wiser beyond our young years. The gay abandonment of youth had given way to a more studious and serious demeanour, in keeping with the seriousness of the life we had just committed to. At this point my mind flickered back to my fellow Novices who had been with me at Erdington and then Perth, but had then decided not to continue. They had gone back to their families and the life they left behind at such a young age. It left me with a feeling of sadness and loss, yet quickly I got my mind together again and began to look forward to my new life.

As the beautiful scenery continued apace and the loveliness became the norm, the miles started to clock up with regularity. By the time seventy miles had passed, on the three hundred plus miles journey, the chit chat became less and less. Some started to doze and then to sleep whilst others just became embroiled in their own sleepy dreams.

The Noviciate at Perth had been exactly one year long. The objective of life at Perth had been to see if the Novices were suitable for the religious life. The next period at Hawkstone Hall in Shropshire, was to be a lengthy and challenging period. The vows we had taken at

Perth were temporary vows and if successful, would be confirmed as permanent after a period of three long years.

In addition, it was necessary for a young Monk with ambitions to become a missionary priest, to endure a lengthy schedule of learning over a six year period, before he could be ordained a Catholic Priest. It was not only necessary to have the desire for Holy Orders, but a trainee must also attain a high level of knowledge and learning, often in excess of that required by a University Graduate.

Hawkstone was known to me and the others through our annual day visits whilst at Erdington. Even so, it was still a daunting move to take, and a giant step into the unknown. My only experiences of Hawkstone Hall, other than the annual Juvenate trips were what we had been told. Each year we would visit the students and play them in a football match, usually with the younger Juvenate boys being the victors. After the match the visitors from Erdington would socialise with the Hawkstone students and have tea before departing for home at Birmingham. This short annual visit was meant to be an introduction for the Juvenists into the lifestyle at Hawkstone, and to meet the more senior members of the religious order, but it hardly prepared them for the harsh realities of life as a Redemptorist student and the six long years of learning to be endured in order for them to be ordained as a priest.
As the coach trundled its way down through the lush green mountains of Cumbria, my thoughts turned to exactly what would be in store for me and the others in our life at Hawkstone. Whilst the time at Perth had been mainly one of work, prayer and integration into the

Monastery life, Hawkstone was all about gaining the knowledge, skill and dedication which would enable me to become a good and successful priest and missionary. It was something of a daunting proposition for someone like me. Unlike my brother I was never an academic and it had so far been a struggle to achieve what I had accomplished. I had never been a quick learner, I failed my eleven plus, and even my seven GCE "O" Levels had been a result of sheer persistence and hard work, rather than any natural ability to learn and absorb. Still I had done it once already, so would I not be able to do it all over again?

The day's journey had been long and arduous, especially without the motorway network of our present day. We were now driving through the lush green pastures of Cheshire and then into rural Shropshire. I began to have a feeling of nervous anticipation but mixed with excitement too. I had never been a person who welcomed change, especially when it was such a seismic change in lifestyle, much preferring what I knew and felt comfortable with.

At last it was almost journey's end. We moved slowly through the beautiful village of Hodnet and then turned slowly through the gates that opened onto a mile long drive to Hawkstone Hall. It seemed to take an age to reach our destination and with rolling farmland on either side of the narrow driveway, it seemed to take an eternity to reach our destination. But finally the coach trundled around the final corner, along the side of the building and around the huge gravel turning circle, before coming to rest on the drive at the front of the magnificent Hawkstone Hall. Tired by the long journey from Perth, we sat in the stationary vehicle for a few moments, and before moving my weary body from my seat, I gazed up at the monumental structure before me. Even though I had visited this place on five or six occasions over the years whilst I was at Erdington, I could not help but be in total awe of the place that I was now privileged to call home, at least for the foreseeable future, and perhaps for life. This was a young boy who came from a council estate in Manchester and from a humble dwelling, yet he was now about to live in a country mansion of immense history, magnificence and enchantment, for who know s how long.

Hawkstone Hall sits within the beautiful green pastures and rolling planes of north Shropshire. It brought to me an image of a diamond set within a magnificent gold band, a jewel surrounded by beautiful clusters of gem stones. From the 18th century onwards, it was widely viewed as one of the principle stately homes of England that attracted visitors from all over Great Britain and beyond.

A building such as this, of such a scale and beauty, can only have been owned by a family from the landed gentry stretching back through many generations. The Hill family, who were descendents from such a line, were first associated with the present Hawkstone's Hall and countryside. They surrounded the superb building by enhancing the natural grace and beauty of the landscape with delightful architecture and country craft that drew people to its agricultural and man made delights. The house was at the centre of an estate that reached out for miles in every direction, containing treasures of natural beauty, further enhanced by the skill and craft of the estate owners during the eighteenth and nineteenth centuries.

Awoken from my daydreams by my brothers leaving the coach, I hurriedly went to collect my single piece of luggage from the hold. I was the last to leave the coach. It belied my comprehension that I was coming to live in such a stately mansion with just a battered leather suitcase containing all of my worldly goods. At first glance, it somehow seemed extremely difficult to reconcile my newly taken vow of poverty with the opulence and grandeur of these new surroundings. The front of the building seemed to span at least a hundred metres in width with two impressive wings jutting out from the mammoth structure. Despite my familiarity with the building and its surroundings, I climbed the steps to the large wooden double doors with a degree of trepidation. It had been one matter to have visited such a place, but to come here and live, perhaps permanently, filled me with a tingling and nervous anticipation. Each emotion had a corresponding and opposite number, for whilst I had a nervous and tentative feeling, bordering on fear, there was also a strong emotion that radiated excitement and the start of a massive life's journey of exploration and fulfilment. Once inside our new home, one of the Brothers came to take my suitcase from me and welcomed me to Hawkstone Hall. I slowly began to take in the size and magnitude of the large communal entrance hall and the beauty of the spacious high ceilings covered end to end in paintings. Likewise the walls were covered in art and murals depicting the splendid history of this mansion. Along with my new fellow students, we were all ushered into the parlour where afternoon tea was served to us before we would be shown to our cells. It was now early evening and the Student's Master entered the parlour as we were finishing our tea. He personally and then formally welcomed all the former Novices to Hawkstone Hall and then one of the senior students was allocated to each of the "newbie's". The students doing this were known as Guardian Angels and their task was to help us to settle in, and then integrate the new recruits into the structure, tradition and rituals of the Redemptorists at Hawkstone.

My "Angel" carried my suitcase-case and ushered me in the direction of what would be my own personal cell. It was very different to the plush formal rooms in the main body of Hawkstone Hall. It was compact, plain and simple as had been my attic cell in the monastery at Perth. It was not in any way in keeping with the style, opulence and great traditions of Hawkstone Hall. In 1926 The Redemptorists, who were a Roman Catholic Missionary congregation, bought the building and much of the land that makes up the Hawkstone Hall Estate. They turned it into a house of higher studies for their students to the priesthood. Much later they built a totally functional block of rooms in the plain style of the 1960's, an oblong block containing three levels, the top two of which created around sixty five bedrooms, in which to house its students and visitors. The ground floor became the new refractory where all of the communal dining would take place.

I was shown to my cell on the second floor which looked inwards towards the rear of the building and the lush green lawns, walkways and garden structures which complemented the mansion house. My cell was plain, on the small side, but quite modern, being decorated in pristine white painted walls and ceilings. It contained a bed, desk, chair and a small set of drawers and a space for hanging my clothes. This was now my home and was comfortable, if a little on the Spartan side. I would be spending many hours each day studying in my cell, so a degree of comfort would be appreciated. After putting away my few belongings, and changing from my travel clothes into my habit, we were all summonsed by the sound of the Church bell calling us to evening prayer. It was all so different to Perth. The Church at Hawkstone was on a much grander scale than the chapel at Perth, and instead of the dozen or so Novices there, the total contingent at Hawkstone numbered around sixty including about thirty five students. After evening prayer we retired to the Refractory where a simple supper was served to the entire company of Priests, Brothers and Religious Students. The final act of the day was recreation time, which would normally be spent in the common room containing books, magazines, games and the like. If the evening was bright and the weather was fair, then the congregation would usually take a late evening stroll around the grounds. As it was a fine September evening, this was a very pleasant way to finish off what had been a long and tiring day. I meandered along with three of my new colleagues taking in the superb gardens, walkways and ponds. We must have wandered around for the best part of an hour which in itself indicates the size and sheer scale of the grounds at Hawkstone Hall. Over the next couple of years I was to spend a lot of my time wandering the gardens and surrounding farmland, where it was quite easy to lose oneself in either quiet relaxation, deep contemplation or just musing about the meaning of life, Hawkstone life, and exactly what I was there to achieve.

When the walk and recreation were over, I walked back into Hawkstone Hall and I took a stroll around the inside of the building. On my several visits to Hawkstone as a Juvenist I had only ever seen a few of the rooms and was not aware of just how splendid it all was. Of course, it had changed from the days when it was privately owned by the landed gentry, but many of the rooms had still retained much of their natural splendour and seemed to be largely untouched since its magnificent heyday in the eighteenth and nineteenth centuries. The Winter Garden was a most beautiful room with a double sided staircase leading both upwards into an entertainment room and downstairs into the cold water plunge. Of course, they had then been altered to suit the requirements of the Redemptorists but its legacy was still one of beauty. The entertainment room was now converted into a study room where I was to spend many hours, days and months in lectures and learning. In the main section of the mansion was the ballroom. It was clear from the opulence of its surroundings and interior décor that this room had hosted many a social event for the gentry in bygone days. The murals on the wall, the fittings and oak panelling tell the story of many a social occasion that still seemed to reverberate around its lavish walls. As I wondered around the Ballroom it was now in dim light and perfectly quiet as if the ghosts of those previous inhabitants were still watching respectfully and possessively over it. I moved quietly through to the adjoining Library which told a thousand tales of year's gone bye. The entire room was bedecked with huge oil paintings and dark oak book shelves which were groaning under the weight of hundreds of books and manuscripts dating back some five hundred years or more. Many were so old that to touch them or pick them up would surely cause them to fall apart at the seams. Some were written in Latin, French or Old English and had clearly not been read, possibly for several centuries. It was a majestic piece of history, although I doubted than many of them would ever see the light of day again. I continued respectfully through all of the public rooms, marvelling as I walked, at the workmanship and quality which had been contained in these rooms for so long. I was still in sheer disbelief that I was permitted to live in such a grand place, and to be a part custodian of so many original works of art.

I meandered back to my cell and just quietly sat in my chair for some several minutes. It was all such a lot to take in at once. After a long and busy day, I was finally alone and left to my own inner thoughts. I found that I did not enjoy being on my own. I felt much better in the company of others and when I was being kept busy. But alone I was, and I slipped quickly into my night clothes, lay my head on the pillows and wondered exactly what tomorrow would bring. I was so used to a rigid routine and knowing exactly what would happen next, but tomorrow would be a leap in the dark, a journey into the unknown and it preyed on my mind.

Sixteen

A New Dawn

Day one arrived in the latest chapter of my new life. The morning bell clanged on the dot of 6am, calling the entire community to morning meditation. After the long tiring journey of the previous day, I could barely drag my weary body out of my bed. It was as much a mental tiredness as a physical one, caused more than likely by the anxiety and anticipation of our new way of life. As always, when the bell tolled, I dropped on my knees by the side of the bed and made an early morning prayer. It was an impromptu reaction to the bell which I had now been listening to for some seven years at Erdington, Perth and now at Hawkstone. I muttered the prayers lowly under my breath, barely thinking about their true meaning, as they had become an almost automatic response to a ringing bell.

The Brothers, Priests and Students all congregated in Church and knelt in the same pew that was designated to them. Habit, repetition and familiarity were very much a feature of monastic life. For half an hour, each and every one of us knelt in silent contemplation or prayer. Who knows, if others felt like I did that particular morning, the session may have been used for a continuation of sleep.

The Monastic breakfast was a routine but adequate meal. Working men required their energy to do their daily tasks and the bread rolls, preserves and coffee were taken in silence once more, so as not to be too easily distracted from the important matters of the new working day ahead.

The most significant difference between the Noviciate at Perth and that of Hawkstone, was that a sizeable portion of each day at my new home was to be spent in study and contemplation. The seminary was a place of learning and many of the students were intellectuals in their own right. Many had come to the Seminary from a University background particularly the older students who had not joined us at the Juvenate at Erdington Abbey.

In order to become a priest, a missionary and a monk, it was essential to have an in-depth knowledge of the required subjects and experience of life itself. It was crucial to be able to impart knowledge and to discuss with authority the key issues of life, of God and his universe. Wisdom was a key requirement. To that date, my seven GCE O Levels seemed somewhat inadequate. Whilst my core subjects in my teenage years had been English, History, French and Geography, I was now about to study and learn the in depth knowledge associated with such deep subjects as Philosophy, Psychology, Latin and Church History. I was about to learn how to preach the Gospel and to give a sermon to hundreds of people listening and latching onto my every word. No pressure then! Most certainly, I knew that I was no scholar. I had worked very hard to achieve my existing qualifications and I was very proud of what I had achieved to-date. In my mind I wondered if perhaps I was more cut out to be a Religious Brother, in a more supportive role, rather than in the front line, in the public eye, as would be a Redemptorist Missionary Priest. Time alone would tell

So after something akin to a sabbatical year in Perth, it was back to the long slog of full time education once more I always detested school and at best I tolerated it. However, I did in fact enjoy my school days, the camaraderie with my school friends, but the actual business of education was not a part of my life that I will recall with any kind of endearment or affection. It was a means to an end, pure and simply, and therefore it had to be endured. Of course, achieving a degree of success helped to enjoy the lessons rather more and I became better and more successful as each term progressed.

Back in the realism of my new situation, I was sat at the back of the class of fourteen students in the rather austere but grand surroundings of my classroom at Hawkstone. My new tutor, who also happened to be the Student Master entered the room and began to tell us that our first lesson was to be in Philosophy. At first, I did not even fully understand the meaning of the word. However, philosophy, according to the Cambridge dictionary is:

"the use of reason in understanding such things as the nature of the real world and existence, the use and limits of knowledge, and the principles of moral judgment:"

The fading memories of my philosophy lessons were that the subject was endeavouring to prove the existence of God and the universe. If I had ever been able to fully understand the logic of the arguments, and I never fully did, then there would have been no reason or need for "belief". As it was, the "philosophy" of proving the existence of God, was not one that I could readily comprehend. Since my age of reason, at around seven years old, I had believed in God and his creation of the world. I had believed because it felt right, and also I was told that it was right. It was not because somebody had proved conclusively that God exists, and that he did indeed create the universe. Like millions of people around our world, belief cannot be shaken by arguments of logic and probability. Belief is the bedrock of any religion.

For just about a full year, I struggled to come to terms with the meaning of philosophy and how to apply it to the meaning of life around me. Father Manson was an extremely clever and educated man and a wonderful priest and person. His knowledge of philosophy was tantamount to being superb. Perhaps he was a brilliant man, and indeed he appeared to be a philosopher himself, but I could never be convinced, even to this day, that he was the best person to teach his subject. To understand knowledge of a subject is one matter, but to impart it, and enable others to learn and understand it, is another skill altogether and Father Manson was not able to do this.

The first day of lessons was something of an ordeal. I had been in Perth and far away from this type of routine and intensity for over a year, and it felt like it. Thankfully, the student classes lasted just for each morning session only, and the afternoons were taken up in more general monastic duties and rituals such as working the farm, tending the gardens, contemplation and a little recreation. Then after afternoon tea, it was back to study once more. Each student would retire to his cell at around 5pm and do private study and "homework" for two and a half hours before evening prayer followed by supper. The difficult part was not just the intensity of the lessons; it was also the loneliness of the time I spent in solitary study. I was not able to work well alone. I had never been a person totally at ease with my own company and I felt the need for more communal interaction with my colleagues.

Fortunately, the Redemptorist Missionary Order was one that incorporated both aspects of the contemplative and missionary life. On the one hand there was the quiet contemplative life in the Monastery and then there was the Missionary work, which was carried out in all types of community, both at home and abroad. I had to become used to, and comfortable, with both aspects of the life.

In my first week at Hawkstone, I was allocated an outside job in the gardens by the Rector. Now I have to confess that I knew absolutely nothing about gardening. I was brought up in a town environment with a meagre garden that my family had at home, when I was young. It was largely made up of clay and weeds and very little else. Mum and Dad were too busy bringing up four children to be gardeners. There was not much chance then for me to tell the difference between a dandelion and a marigold except that both are orange coloured, and I did not even know that at the time. I was really quite pleased then, when I was told that my daily afternoon job each day was the care of the rear lawns. When I say lawns, I should really say football pitches, because the lawns were huge, and they were as close to being a bowling green in appearance, as I had seen. It was surprising then that my lawn mower was of the "push" variety and with a rotary action, so it relied entirely on "pushing" it in absolutely straight lines for hour after hour in order to achieve a quarter inch finish. The lawns were to become my pride and joy, so much so that I did not even like to see the community walking on them in case it ruined the beautiful striped appearance. The Centre Court at Wimbledon would have been proud to call the lawns their own! With such extensive and lush green garden lawns, I would spend many, many hours walking slowly in straight lines, up and down, my head bowed. My fellow Brothers may have thought that I was deep in contemplation, and perhaps that was the case, but it was also so that I could make parallel and crisscross lines across the beautiful and coiffured lawns. Care of the lawns was to be my therapy!

This job was to become my saviour. The new lifestyle at the seminary was very different to anything that I had previously experienced before. I was already struggling to come to terms with the difficult morning study sessions. In addition, I found the long periods of solitude and silence were against my natural inclinations and the evening study times were lengthy and tiresome. The same question was always at the back, and sometimes at the forefront of my mind. Was this the life for me? Was I cut out to live the life of a monk, of a Catholic priest, of a missionary? As had been the case for the past three years, there was to be no definitive answer at that time.

My afternoon sessions then, as lawn-maker in chief, were something that kept me sane and reasonably content. The time spent pushing my lawn mower was indeed spent in contemplation and prayer, from time to time. I would speak to God as if he was my Father or a close friend. I believed that I was in close personal contact with him and I spoke to him in normal and real English. I genuinely believed that I had been called to serve God and live my life doing his will, and to help others. During this time I would also think about everything from the meaning of life, my studies, the City football result or what we were about to have for supper. After all, we were normal human people, were we not, with normal feelings, desires and ambitions but leading an abnormal life, by any standards.

One autumnal morning I awoke, and as was my want, I would pull back the curtains to admire my beautifully cultured lawns. Instead I was horrified to see pile upon pile of soil hills cutting a swathe across my pride and joy! Was this sabotage? Was one of my brothers trying to score points against me? Well no! I quickly dressed before morning meditation and inspected the suspect soil parcels. It became evident quite quickly, even to a "non-gardener" of a gardener like me, that we had been attacked by a colony of moles. I found it difficult to concentrate during meditation and mass that day, and my mind kept wondering to the garden instead of keeping my mind on my prayers. I hurried through my breakfast and before 7.30am that morning I was out and inspecting the damage, wondering what I could do to rescue the situation before the rest of this lawn and all the other lawns, came under a "mole attack" too. As a "townie" with very little experience of gardening, other than my one year in Perth, I knew that I had to obtain some expert advice. That help came in the shape of one Brother Thomas. He had been part of the Redemptorist Order for well over 60 years and was now in the twilight of his life. His health was now very poor, and his time now was spent mostly in his cell reading, or in quiet contemplation of life and beyond. I knew that he had a wealth of experience in farm work and gardening and I approached him for help. I was barely twenty years old and he was well into his eighties. He was delighted to help. I think that people very rarely asked for his opinion or help anymore and he could not wait to help me rid my lawns of these pesky little blighters! It was a strange relationship that developed between us over the next two years. He was a man of great experience of life, albeit from a narrow perspective, and me, still wet behind the ears and barely twenty two years old. My knowledge of life seemed like nothing by comparison. In the outside world, such a relationship would rarely be seen and would not work, and yet, I would love spending time in his company and listening to his fascinating tales and experiences and taking advice from him as if he were my Grandfather. Perhaps he had become a kind of surrogate Grandfather as I had lost both my real Grandparents on my maternal and paternal sides, by the time I was two years old. Brother Thomas took me to the farm shed where he pulled out a quantity of mole traps. Clearly this had been a problem on the farm or in the gardens before. He explained to me how a colony of moles would burrow down about twelve inches below the surface and would then create a labyrinth of tunnels from home to home. After each burrowing session, the mole would have a pile of unwanted earth to move after creating its run. It would tunnel the only way it could, upwards and out through the lawn in order to create a soil mountain. This would be repeated all along the grass in the line of the tunnel. It was clearly a very clever and effective way to build a home. It was very good for the moles, but not so good for the poor gardener and people who wanted to see pristine lawns. The solution according to Brother Thomas was simple and clinical. *"You've got to catch them and kill them"* he said, without emotion. I am not sure why I was surprised by that. I thought perhaps that such a simple, gentle and holy man would know of a way to discourage them from damaging the lawns without actually killing them. But no, he showed me a dozen mole traps that he had no doubt used on the farmland before, which trap the mole inside a tube that is placed into the tunnel. As the mole enters the tube, a strong spring snaps down onto its head and breaks its neck resulting in [mercifully], instant death. From my only ever experience of moles, in a nature magazine, I believed them to be cute, furry creatures, so why would we want to hurt them? I had also learned that moles are completely blind and do not have eyes. They were hardly vermin and I did not feel good about killing them if it was not absolutely necessary for the care of my lawns. Still, I had no choice, the lawns were being ruined and so I went along with Brother Thomas's advice and laid the trap. The next morning I went to see the result. I dug down into the tunnel where I had placed the trap, and I found what I did not want to find. I wanted to see the trap empty, but sure enough, in the trap, dead with a broken neck, was a beautiful, small furry mole. It was totally different to catching a rat in a trap. I could never have handled a rat. I released the little fellow from the trap and put it into my hand. I decided there and then that I would not kill any more of these wonderful little creatures. Was it just sentimental rubbish? Yes I'm sure it was, but even so, I had another plan. I amended the traps to take out the spring mechanism and then I re-set them. Sure enough, the next time I looked into the trap, there was a live mole which I quickly transferred into a box. I must have walked a mile or more before releasing him into another part of the estate. I imagine that they probably had a homing device of some sort and that they would make their way back down to the gardens and wreak their havoc once more. Then, I repeated the process each time I caught a mole, and about ten times afterwards, until they stopped coming into the traps. I had released them alive into farmland some distance away. It may have been a fool's errand as they may have found their way back, but for the time being my lawns were mole free. I never told Brother Thomas of my sentimental decision to set them free. I just thought it would be better if we just left it that way.

From that time onwards, I would occasionally seek out the company of this lovely octogenarian. I admired him greatly. He was a simple and a holy man but very worldly and funny in many ways. When walking out together in the gardens, I was this twenty one year old with his eighty something year old companion, we must have looked very much "the odd couple" but it was him that kept me grounded and able to continue with my life at Hawkstone.

On one particular occasion, Brother Thomas was ill and confined to his cell. I visited him there and we talked about all manner of topics. He was not a self centred man and he would always enquire as to how I was getting along, and ask if he could give me any help, advice or support. I was very much an open book and could not mask my feelings well at all. He was very much aware that I was finding life at Hawkstone to be extremely challenging and that I was struggling on both an academic and emotional front. The truth was that I had the ability to succeed on the academic subjects, but I was neither motivated nor emotionally able to study sufficiently, to be able to master the subjects. Brother Thomas took a "Fatherly" nay "Grand-fatherly" stance in trying to steer me through those troubles waters. On one occasion I remember asking him about himself. He knew that he was ill and that he did not have very long to live, and I had been bold enough to ask him a deeply searching question. *"Brother Thomas,"* I ventured almost apologetically, *"are you absolutely sure that there is a God up there waiting for you?"* I knew that he would not have been offended by the question or he would not have answered! Immediately he snapped back: *"I b****y well expects so, or I've just wasted sixty five years!"* It was hardly swearing, but I had never heard him use "industrial" language before so I was somewhat taken aback. Clearly, despite his strong and unwavering belief, he still had a slight element of doubt about life after he would depart this earth. It must have been only a mater of weeks before it became clear that Brother Thomas was spending his last few days on earth. The Superiors had drawn up a rota of times when the community could visit and this was limited to just a few per day and for short periods only. I was one of the most junior members and by the time I had my opportunity to visit him, he had slipped into a state of unconsciousness. I had really hoped to have spoken to him one last time before he died, as there was unfinished business between us. The second question that I had asked him on an earlier occasion was an impertinent one, but I knew that he would not take offence and that he would still answer me:

"Brother Thomas, if you do go to heaven and meet God, will you come back and tell me, or will you at least let me know, somehow?" He laughed out loud and said to me: *"I will do my very best, if God will allow me!"*

As he lay there, his breathing very shallow, I held his hand tightly. This was a man with whom I had built a close relationship, as close as anybody was supposed to be, within a Religious Order. I was not a member of his birth family, but I was still a member of his extended religious family. I had spent time with him, when he was well, and we would discuss all manner of things about life, the Redemptorists, and his wealth of experience as a Religious Brother. Although he was barely conscious, I felt within me that he knew I was there with him. The hand squeeze was mainly mine, but I honestly felt as if he was squeezing my hand back in response." It was a feeling I cannot ever forget. I really wanted him to know that I was there at his end and I genuinely believe he did.

After he was gone, I missed Brother Thomas greatly. I seemed to be able to develop friendly relationships with older people, more so than with my younger associates. Perhaps I needed the guiding hand of their great experience in life. Similarly, I had forged other good relationships with an older Brother at Perth. They knew so much about life and yet they were so humble and simple. They were completely honest and transparent in what they did and there was no hidden agenda. Without Brother

Thomas I had lost my friend, my guiding hand, my confidante, and I missed his sound advice and his ability to keep my spirits high when I was feeling very low.

Many of the Brothers were real characters. As an aspiring young man trying to become a priest, it was sometimes easy to underestimate the role of the "Brother." They did not seek the public limelight and they just quietly went about their work without fuss. The Brothers were Redemptorists, but their role was to support the work of the Priests who were involved with people in the parish or on the retreats and missions. The Brothers were quite content to take a back seat role and support the missionary effort by doing all the jobs that kept the monastery working. The jobs they did included cooking, general maintenance, and farming, playing the organ, and cleaning. In fact, whatever work that needed doing in the monastery or in the grounds was done by the brothers. It was not because they were any less educated or clever. In fact it was my privilege to often learn many things from them. Some were normal men who wanted to live the simple life. Others were well educated and very intelligent people who preferred the life of the Brother to that of the front line Priest and Missionary. I remember well, playing chess with one of the Brothers at recreation time in the Common Room. I never confessed to being a good player, but I did not expect to be so comprehensively beaten by this particular Brother. He won the match by five games to nil and won each game within a just a few minutes. I naturally congratulated him on his win. He just shrugged his shoulders and with a huge smile he just said: *"I got lucky today, you'll win the next match."* I took him up on his comment and tried again a couple of weeks later. Despite all my best efforts, the end result was much the same. I did not play him again, it was too one sided a contest. He needed somebody who was able to give him a challenging game. He must have been a "Ringer". If not, he was just a "Chess" genius.

Whoever taught Brother Thomas his Chess must have been a good player and perhaps it was Brother Aden. Now besides being an absolute wiz at Chess, Brother Aden was one to avoid at cards. Quite frequently at recreation time, particularly when the weather was wet, or it was dark, a number of the students and brothers would play cards. Naturally, having all taken a vow of poverty there was no money involved in the stakes, so they generally played for other items such as buttons or rosary beads. Some of the games played were Whist and Black Jack, but Brother Aden always wanted to play Poker, he was extremely competitive, and he would take it very seriously. I don't think that I ever saw him lose a game in the years that I was at Hawkstone. Rumour has it that before he joined the Redemptorists, [he joined in later life], that he was a member of the SAS in the armed forces. Now that would have explained a lot!

Seventeen

The Redemptorist Way

There were so many facets to the life of a Redemptorist Priest, Monk or Brother. I think perhaps that this was the thing that attracted me to the Order in the first place. I was just aged eleven when my parents took me along with my elder brother to a Religious Exhibition. There were dozens of different Religious Organisations, all trying to attract young people to join their order. There were Parish Priests, Contemplative Orders and all types of Missionary Orders vying with one another to recruit their next generation of ministers from the ranks of these youngsters

I am not exactly sure what it was that drew me to the Redemptorists. It could even have been the long black habit that looked so smart with its Rosary Beads draped along its thick black belt. It may even have been the warm outdoor cape, along with the hood, that gave off something of a mystical presence to the monk wearing it. Whatever it was, it was very persuasive to an eleven year old boy. I remember thinking at the time about the excitement of being sent out to Africa to preach the Missions, to the poor black people, who were in need of conversion to God. It could have been the Missionary visits preaching to other Parishes in Britain, or it could also have been the mysterious Monasteries in which the members of the Order were housed. Whatever simple reason it was that attracted me to it, I knew at the time that it was the Order of Redemptorists that I wanted to join.

At Hawkstone, it was essential for me to develop the wisdom and knowledge of all matters religious, so that I could preach the word with knowledge and authority. The studying and learning I found particularly arduous. I was much more at home in the more practical aspects of the training to be a priest. One of these was the skill to preach to a congregation or to any group of people who wanted to learn about the ministry. I was particularly keen to be a Missionary after I had passed my final examinations and qualified to be a monk and then a priest. The attraction about becoming a Redemptorist is that I could get to do both, as part of the life was Contemplative, and part was Missionary. In the future there could be periods when I may be told to spend six months or more in the quiet life of a Monastery and then perhaps a year outside the Monastery on the Missions. Of course, having taken a vow of obedience, it was not up to me what I would do. It was to be the decision of my superiors. I would be given a role to carry out and that is what I would have to do, and without complaint, whether it was to my liking or not.

One of the practical lessons we had to learn was the art of giving a sermon. It is not everybody that is cut out to be a preacher, and I have heard some excellent sermons in my time and some pretty awful and boring sermons over the years. Fortunately, I felt that I had something of a natural gift of preaching, and I always felt comfortable and in control when I was doing any kind of public speaking. Even so, it was nerve wracking to have to stand in a pulpit in front of all my peers, colleagues and other members of the Religious Order and preach a pre-written sermon to them, with true belief, sincerity and a genuine conviction.

When I had to give my debut sermon, even though it was only a training session, I would have felt more at home if I had been able to use my own words, something I had written myself. I would then have been able to do so with genuine conviction and belief. As it was, I was asked to give a pre-prepared sermon written by a preacher from many years ago, even hundreds of years before. These sermons were taken from a book of classic sermons from great Redemptorist preachers of the past. It was quite unnerving therefore, to preach a sermon to my colleagues and contemporaries, when the sermon subject was all about sin and hell! Although the 1970's were supposed to be enlightened years in the new modern age, here I was preaching a sermon about fire and brimstone, sin, hell and damnation. However, this was what I was asked to do, and so I did so. The actor that was within me, enabled me to put great feeling into the way I preached the sermon and I gave out a powerful rendition which I believe was extremely strong, authoritative and with great conviction. At the end of my sermon, my superiors and my colleagues gave a critique of my performance and most of them were very complimentary. I felt inside of me, that I had what it took to give a really good and convincing sermon.

When I had time to reflect, I was concerned about the subject matter we had used. Even though it was just a practice, a training session in the art of preaching, I was somewhat traumatised about the words I had used and the teachings that the Catholic Church had put forward as "Gospel" truth, only a few short decades ago. From my time spent at Erdington and Perth, I believed that the teaching on heaven, hell and purgatory were still widely held beliefs among the Catholic public at large.

I was pleased that my colleagues had thought that I could become a good preacher, but I was not happy with the subject I had spoken. It was all too close for comfort. Even as a young boy, just a few short years before, I had been scared, even traumatised, when listening to priests giving sermons about sin. It seemed to me that just about everything one could do was a sin, and the teaching of the Church at that time, was that if a person died in a state of mortal sin, then that person would go to hell. This was the teaching I was brought up with and it seemed to me at the time, that it was about a God to fear, rather than a God of love and forgiveness. In my young mind I could understand that a murderer who died without confessing his sin would go to hell, but I could not understand how failing to go to Mass on a Sunday would result in that person going to hell for ever and eternity.

As a young child, we had been taught that Hell was the place that a person would go to, when he or she died, if they died whilst in a state of mortal sin. If that person confessed the sin to a priest and sought forgiveness, no matter how terrible the crime, then God would forgive that person, who would then go to heaven when they died. If however, that person died before seeking forgiveness then he or she would go to Hell, which would mean living for an eternity without being with God. Hell was the place that Lucifer, The Devil, was sent to when he rejected God. Hell to us meant an eternity, spent forever without God, without his happiness, and in the burning fires of Hell!

By the time I had arrived at Hawkstone, the emphasis on teaching about Hell had changed somewhat and the focus was on love, forgiveness and Heaven. But in my mind, the truth was the truth, and it does not alter just because of a change of leadership or of fashion. If Hell is a reality and is the truth, then how can that change and why would it not be the truth any longer?

These were the worries and contradictions that would prey on my young mind, and they did not want to go away. Whilst at the senior seminary, these issues were there in my subconscious and were unresolved. Perhaps if I had raised the subject during Philosophy lessons, then there may have been an answer that would have satisfied my fears, but I did not do so, because to do so may have seemed like heresy, in questioning a teaching that had been part of the bedrock of Christian teaching for hundreds of years and although rarely mentioned these days, I believe that it still is.

There was one particular occasion when I came very close to questioning the teaching of the Church on this particular issue. It was at one of our regular practice sessions for preaching sermons. For the newer students, [and I was still in my first year at Hawkstone at the time,] we had to practice our sermons using the material of other Redemptorists from previous generations. These had been compiled into books and many of the sermons must have dated back some two or three hundred years. The thinking at that time was much more severe than it is nowadays and the preaching was very much about keeping people in line, by the teaching of fear of God more than the love of

God. The sermons at the time were full of strict rules and told of what would happen to members of the congregation should they not adhere to them. Nowadays, there is very little, if hardly ever mention of hell when preaching the Catholic faith and the emphasis is on love.

I gave my sermon to my colleagues. It was a powerful sermon with a lot of material dealing with sin and hell and the consequences for people not obeying the Ten Commandments. It was strong stuff! It was certainly not the kind of sermon you would hear these days in either Roman Catholic or any of the Christian Churches.

At the end of my sermon there was the usual critique, more about style, presentation and performance, because the content, of course, was not mine. In the critique, one of the older Priests commented positively on my style and presentation, but he made a point of saying that I needed to put more conviction into what I was saying. I thought about the comments for a few moments and then I replied: *"I think I could have showed more conviction if I had really believed in what I was saying"*. There was a silence and then the Priest said: *"Well, there is more emphasis on the love of God nowadays"*. The words said it all.

Eighteen

Life at Hawkstone

Despite all the other facets of monastic life at Hawkstone, it was learning and study that were the key elements of our life there. It was to take six long years of study and education before qualification as a priest would be achieved. The main subjects were to be Philosophy, Psychology, Church History and Bible studies. In addition, there were many other arts and skills that I had to master in order to carry out the duties of being a Monk and a Priest. Among the most important were Teaching, Preaching, Mass, Confessions, and Counselling. When compared to the average University Student, who would major two or three topics, the student priest had a huge portfolio of subjects to master, before he was able to practice these skills on his congregation and parishioners.

As previously hinted at, whilst I felt able to master the skills of various key subjects, I was struggling to cope with the demands of Philosophy in particular. At the end of each term, there would be in depth examinations to assess the learning of each student. In one such end of term philosophy examination, I had such a mental blank that I was barely able to give a coherent answer to the majority of the questions. The exam time permitted was two hours, but before the end of one hour, I had completed all the information that I was able to give. I had not provided full and complete answers to the questions. I put down my pen, and then laid my uncompleted exam papers on my desk and left the room. I knew it had been a complete and utter disaster. I was the only person to leave the room before the end of the examination. I questioned my own reasons for not understanding and mastering the topic, but deep down I knew the reasons why. I knew that I had not been able to study sufficiently in order to master the topic of philosophy, but the reason I had not done so, was because I was emotionally unable to concentrate on study, when I knew that I had deeper and more pressing problems. Deep inside me, although I could not admit it to myself, I was then seriously unhappy at Hawkstone, it had affected my ability to study, and I very much doubted that I could continue further and to the end of the process.

The expected call came from my Philosophy tutor, Fr. Patrick Manson. He was a brilliant and learned man, but his understanding of people often left a lot to be desired. I was called into his office the day after the philosophy examination and was asked to explain why I had left the room before completing the papers. I could not give him a satisfactory answer, other than I did not know the answers to the questions. I told him that I was finding it difficult to understand Philosophy, but I did not tell him that the real reason for the failure was my inability to spend the time studying the subject and to concentrate on it. He was unable to realise that there were deeper reasons involved, and so he merely insisted that I re-sit the examination after one month. This would, he told me, give me time to study philosophy more, but that if I failed, I would be unable to be ordained a priest. I could not allow that to happen. I therefore spent all my available time during the following month, doing my absolute utmost to make the grade in philosophy. I spent all the evening study periods on this one subject, possibly to the detriment of my other subjects and I also spent much of my free time working on it too. Eventually, a month had passed by, and Fr. Manson set aside an afternoon for me to re-take the examination. It felt strange to sit in a large room, all on my own and to start the examination all over again. Although philosophy did not come easily to me, I had remembered the main questions from the previous papers and had concentrated my answers on the last examination. I did finish the job this time. I spent all two hours permitted and completed answers to all of the questions. The following day, he came to see me and told me that I had met the grade and passed the examination.

I should have felt elated, or at least pleased, but instead I felt flat. The truth was that I no longer felt that I wanted to be there any longer. If I was to fail to reach my ambition to be a priest at Hawkstone, it was certainly not going to be because of a failed philosophy examination. It would have to be my decision, my decision only, and taken for all the right reasons, but not because of failing an exam.

The following months became more and more difficult. The academic demands and the study made my life in the monastery unhappy and less fulfilling. At this point I had now spent over a year in Shropshire at the Seminary and I was beginning to question my reasons for being there and whether my future was to be a Redemptorist Priest? There were many good reasons for continuing my life there, but also, I was beginning to feel very unsure of myself and what my future held. I had lost my confidence and desire.

At times when I felt particularly down and unsettled, I would think of all the good reasons why I should just carry on regardless and complete what I had set out to do.

My first reason was that I still believed that I had been called to the priesthood and that I was a chosen one. It was not something that anybody would easily reject. On the other hand, perhaps I was mistaken and I had not received a calling. Then, and most importantly, was the feeling of gratitude to my parents and family for the sacrifices they had made, to enable me to set out on this fantastic journey. I would then think about the ten years that I had already spent out of my young life, going along this path to Priesthood. I would think about the fantastic places that I had been privileged to call my home. There was the beautiful monastery at Erdington where I had genuinely enjoyed my early school days despite the ongoing questions in my mind. The monastery at Perth was a wonderful place to live and I had been kept there at the expense of the Order, when I contributed nothing to my keep there. And then to come to beautiful Shropshire and to live in the stately mansion at Hawkstone Hall was a wonderful thing, and I truly appreciated how lucky I was and how privileged I had been, to call these places my home. Why would I not be happy? At times like these I would think to myself just what I would be doing if I were not a member of the Order of the Redemptorists. I was now in my early twenties and my fine education to-date was academic, but what would I do with my life if I were not here? Again, it was a question I was unable to answer at that particular moment in time as the answer eluded me.

Over the coming weeks and months I began to spend a lot more time on my own. This in itself was not that unusual as it was indeed something of a solitary life even when living with fifty or more people. Silence had always been a key part of being a Redemptorist. It was still very easy to feel alone in such a huge house and with such extensive and beautiful gardens and grounds. The intensity and pressure of the life indoors, the studies, meditation, prayers and training, led me to seek more and more time outside of the monastery where it was peaceful and I felt more at ease with life and relaxed, even though it could also be solitary and lonely.

The gardens to the rear of the house were extensive. In addition to the cultivated lawns and flowered areas, there was also a large woodland area which was littered with religious grottos and statues. It was serene just to walk peacefully, alone with my own thoughts, through the wooded area along the rough pathways surrounded by ancient and gnarled trees, many of which were hundreds of years old. If they could have spoken, they would have many a story to tell about people from previous generations walking by them. It made me think that our own brief lives are so short and insignificant by comparison. The only noises to be heard were from the birds which were housed in the trees and the odd scuffle of wildlife in the undergrowth, perhaps a mouse or a pheasant and the odd fox. The cultivated woodland gave way to a lovely and very large man made lake, which had been built just the previous year. I was proud to be able to say that along with several of my other brothers, I had dug out and created this lovely lake, a masterpiece, which was now the home to lilies, all kind of water foliage and was now inhabited by frogs, fish and all types of water life. Despite its relative youth, the lake melted into its surroundings and looked as if it had been there for many generations. It had now become the permanent home for a colony of ducks and the occasional home to visiting migratory birds such as Canadian Geese and their like. I would often linger around the lake thinking "this lake is partly down to me," and marvel at the serenity of it all.

Moving on from the lake, I would move onto the quiet cemetery area. It was the place where the Redemptorists buried its own dead. Strangely, I did not find it a sad place. The priests, monks and brothers who were now resting there, had all lived their lives usefully and had now moved on. The plots were all in the same identical style: A simple white cross with an inscription showing their name, title, date of birth, date of vows and their date of death. It also showed the number of years that they had been a priest, brother or monk. The cemetery was in a single line backing onto a walled vegetable garden which produced much, if not all of the fruit and vegetables for the dinner table. It was such a beautiful place, and started with the most recently deceased and went along the single line to the oldest who had died dating back to 1926 when the Redemptorists first arrived at Hawkstone Hall. Half way along the line of graves, was a small break and a path leading to a large rustic gate that led me into the walled garden. Inside was a totally enclosed space and huge in its proportions. In its heyday, this walled garden had to feed an extended family and guests of the gentry all year round, with all manner of fruit and vegetables. Now, at this time, it had to do a similar job. The Order of the Redemptorists had to be self sufficient. Its only income was from the missionary work, pastoral Courses and seminars, for which it was paid, and by donations from benefactors. In order to maintain a large property such as Hawkstone Hall, it was necessary to earn a regular income, in order to balance the books, and by being as self sufficient as possible. Food self sufficiency was a major contributory factor, even for the simple life-style of the Redemptorists. So the walled gardens were prepared by the Brothers so as to provide fruit and vegetables all year round for the community's table. To complete the food self sufficiency, the Brothers used to work the adjoining small farm where milk and eggs were produced daily. Ultimately, the sheep and cows, as well as providing milk, would contribute to the self sufficiency when sold at the nearby farmers markets, in order to provide food.

I had been brought up in the town, so for me it was a pleasure to be involved in food production and farming, if only as an onlooker or occasional helper. I would often spend time walking around the walled gardens and the farm, and I would stop to talk or pass the time of day with the Brothers who worked on it. The role of the Redemptorist Brothers should never be underestimated. Their role was an understated one and was to support the Priests in their Missionary work. They would keep out of the public eye and set about their daily jobs quietly and efficiently whether on the farms or working around the monastery. They played a supportive and superlative role, and one which was essential to the good running of the Monastery, the farm, the land, and for the community.

To the front of Hawkstone Hall, the grounds of the Mansion had many memorable and magnificent features and surprises. The history of the house and its estate dates back to the middle ages, but the last known descendant of the Hawkstone family, John of Hawkeston, died in 1467.

A long, winding private road meanders up the hill with green pastures on either side. It is not used for cars, and is for the use of agricultural vehicles only, in order to access the beautiful fields and farmland. Down the rolling fields to the right is the magnificent Hawk Lake. In 1784 work began on the formation of the lake, a long and narrow stretch of water. It was designed to be a navigable river. It is two miles long and this serpentine took three years to construct. Hawke Lake no longer belongs to Hawkstone Hall, but in its day it produced all the requirements for fishing to the gentry, and river food for the Hall's inhabitants. Beyond the serpentine is the ruin of an ancient Abbey which was part of grounds at the time. At the top of the hill and over the horizon lies, what is now known as the Grotto. It cannot be seen from the Hall and is a good mile's walk from it. From a huge rock, caverns were hewn into Grotto Hill. The Victorian's treated this as a folly and would walk among them with lanterns. Many were the days that I would take a long walk out from Hawkstone, sometimes alone and at other times with my Brothers. We would walk through the caves with only candles to give us the light to see our way ahead even in daytime. Nowadays, the caves at Hawkstone are a major tourist attraction in the area and are no longer part of the estate.

I would frequently walk to the outskirts of the estate, mostly alone to one of my favourite places. It was somewhat over a mile from the Hall and over farmland. It was a place where I could find peace and quiet and magnificent splendour. I had never really loved my own company very much, but there were times back then, when I sought out solitary places, where I could go alone, just to be at home with my own thoughts. My deepest thoughts were not the type that I felt I could share with my Brothers at Hawkstone, and so I kept my own counsel

It was a Monument on the edge of the estate, erected in 1795 to commemorate Sir Rowland Hill, a former Lord Mayor of London, who bought the manor of Hawkstone in the year 1549. The monument was built of red and white sandstone, a product of the local area, and it stands to a height of 112 feet on the terrace. The statue which stands above the pillar and the viewing area represents Sir Rowland Hill in his Lord Mayor's robes. The statue was toppled from its fine perch during a storm in 1935, but a new statue replaced it in 1991 during the restoration of the attractions of Hawkstone Park. The surrounding countryside is so high that the monument seemed to tower much higher than its 112 feet. It was a steep climb to the summit, but as a twenty one year old, I could almost run up the spiral stone stairs to the top and back down again, without even breaking breath. When I was at the summit and walking nervously around its narrow perimeter, I could see the whole of Shropshire and up-to twelve surrounding counties, weather permitting, and marvelled at the peace and quiet of such a beautiful view. I would gaze down towards Hawkstone Hall and it would look like a piece of monopoly property, from the board game. From my perfect isolation so high up, I would wonder about my life and where it would go from there. This monument was my solitary place and I do not remember ever seeing another person there during my entire time at Hawkstone. It was almost as if it was my place and mine alone. In a strange manner, I had become completely attached and attracted to this wonderful tower and yet it also had bad feelings too. How could I ever leave this magical place called Hawkstone, it was a place I loved and loathed, and yet how much longer would I be able to call it my home?

Over the passing months, I became more and more withdrawn and isolated. It was as if I was withdrawing into a shell to protect myself from the outside world. I was doing all the same things that everybody else was doing in terms of communal activity, and so nobody would have noticed that I had begun to feel alone and not really a part of what was going on. It was strange to live in such close proximity to so many people and yet not to have a close relationship with any other person. I had not told anybody how I felt about my life there, about any worries or anxieties and likewise none of my colleagues ever confided in me as to how they felt about their life. To all intents and purposes, all the other Brothers seemed to be perfectly happy and content. Perhaps I was the only one who was having any deliberations about their future?

A lot of time would be spent each day in the Church for Mass, meditation and other services, and yet quite often I would just go alone into the church and sit in a rear pew and just think. Often, the Brother who practiced the organ music would be there playing. I loved the sound of organ music and I would frequently just sit and listen, think about things and pray, often for quite a long period.

There were times when I would spend a lot of time outdoors either in the gardens or walking in the fields. I found that time spent inside the monastery was intense and formal, whatever activity I was partaking in and I would welcome any opportunity to be outside and taking part in other activities. I really enjoyed mixing with the outside community although these times were few and far between. One of the activities I really enjoyed and gave me great fulfilment was in teaching the catechism to local schoolchildren. It was also a part of my training to teach and impart knowledge to others and I would feel much more at home in doing this. Each Wednesday evening, once a week, I would cycle some seven or eight miles to one of the local villages, where I would teach catechism to some young people. In the countryside, Catholic Churches were few and far between and many of the local children were unable to attend a school where religious Education was part of the curriculum. I would spend half an hour with two young people and talk to them about the bible and the stories of the Catechism. It was worth a sixteen mile cycle ride to Shawbury to do something worthwhile and to obtain some fulfilment from doing so. Perhaps it was a form of escapism from the daily grind of study and normal monastic activity. I was always a gregarious kind of person, and yet I desperately needed company, and so I used to seek out the kind of activity that best suited me.

When an opportunity arose to teach the Catechism to another group of children I was the first to volunteer. As I was already going to Shawbury every Wednesday evening, I also took on another class on a Monday evening with a different group of children in a village not too far away. For me, I found it as a form of escapism from the daily monastery routine. I used to love mingling with the community, the children and their parents. The job had been given to me by the Rector but the Novice Master must not at first have realised that I was out of the Monastery on two evenings of every week. When he became aware, he decided to make a change. He came to see me in my cell one evening as I was studying. He asked me if I enjoyed taking the Catechism classes. I told him that I enjoyed it very much and that I got great satisfaction out of teaching the children. He then told me that whilst he was very pleased with the job I had been doing, that he was going to give the task to another of the students. He said to me: *"Brother, I want you to concentrate now on your studies and I am giving the Catechism class to Brother Tony."* I did not let my emotions show. I knew that I had to accept his decision without complaint or question. Yet, inside of me, I was crest-fallen; doing the Catechism classes had given me a real motivation but more importantly, it enabled me to spend some time outside of Hawkstone. I was beginning to feel confined, as I had been in Perth. My two evenings in the community teaching Catechism was what I felt I needed, and it was what I was good at, but Father Manson believed that it was hindering my studies and that I was falling behind the other students. He may have been correct in that respect and yet his decision to make me spend more time back at

Hawkstone and in studying, was to have a seriously detrimental affect on my overall performance and my ability to make the grade as a Missionary Priest.

Close by the Seminary at Hawkstone, there was a cottage within the grounds which was the home of a local family who worked on the farm. Over a period of time I became quite friendly with them and used to go and visit them when I had spare time. I would go and see them and chat to them sometimes for hours. They were very familiar with the Hawkstone students and I enjoyed spending time in their company. As time went along, I had spent an increasing amount of my time with them, and although we both enjoyed it, they eventually gave me the impression that I was going there too often. I could feel it in the things that they would say, and I then began to realise that I may have been also using them as a form of escapism, although I had not realised that I was doing so. I believe that what really appealed to me, but only in my subconscious, was the family environment. It was beginning to dawn on me that I was a sociable and gregarious person and that I was finding it difficult to spend long periods of my life in silence and on my own. The family environment was what I was missing and I had begun to seek it out, both by visiting this family and in the Catechism classes that I had been so keen to take part in. Once that I realised what was happening, I stopped visiting the farm and I just passed the time of day when I saw the members of the family. I never explained to them why I had stopped going but they must have wondered.

For me to stop visiting the family at the farm was yet

another severe blow to my confidence. I had been unwittingly using the catechism classes and the visits to the farm to help me get by, to give me a feeling of a normal family life instead of the community life. I was using them as a means of keeping my sanity. I found that I enjoyed and needed the company of these other people and that being in the Monastery so much of the time, was making me feel increasingly depressed, somewhat isolated and questioning if I still wanted to be there. I was unsure how I would manage now that these two avenues of "escapism" were being closed to me. Inside of me, I still wanted to fulfil my ambition and become a Priest but more and more, I was finding it difficult to live the life in the manner that was being expected of me by my superiors.

Nineteen

The Downward Spiral

I had been at Hawkstone Hall for almost two years and it was the spring of 1969. The time had seemed to pass by very slowly, but I had since settled into the life at Hawkstone, just as I had done previously at Erdington and Perth. It was not without misgivings and difficulties. All three places were great institutions and with hindsight, I had become institutionalised whilst in each of those places. I had slotted into the routines and rituals like a chameleon, because I had not known anything different. It was what I had been brought up to do, and I was in my tenth year with the Redemptorists. I was being carried along on a very powerful tide and it was almost impossible to get off without being injured. It was something like a huge Roller Coaster. I had enjoyed the ride up-to a point, but it was also very scary and it was going so fast, that it would have been far more difficult to get off, than to hang on and get safely to the end of the ride. And that is how I felt for most of my time there. If only I had known at that time, that some of my colleagues and brothers felt the same as I did, then I may have had the strength to do something about it, but each and every one of us had been brought up with a type of stoicism, whereby we kept our council and did not share our thoughts and feelings with each other. This was always likely to be the case as we were encouraged to treat everyone the same and never to become close to any individual, or make friends with any particular brother. It was a strange journey that I was set upon. I sometimes loved it and sometimes I hated it. I had also lost good friends along the way. The large majority of my school friends back at Erdington had long since left and started another life back in Civvy-street. Several of my friends had also departed once they arrived at the Noviciate at Perth. Strangely, since I had arrived at Hawkstone almost two years earlier, none of my colleagues who had travelled with me from Perth had left the order and neither did they give any inclination that they were planning to do so. Like me, on the surface, all was well with the world however who was to know what was going on underneath the surface and in their minds. Only time alone would tell.

To the outside world, many of our activities in the seminary may have seemed strange and unusual, things such as meditation, confessions, periods of silence and the like. On the other hand, there were many activities in our Seminary life that were quite usual and would give an air of seeming normality. We would play football each week. We had a football pitch in the grounds and there were some thirty five to forty healthy young men with plenty of energy to burn. Our only outside fixture each year would be against the Juvenate boys from Erdington, but there would be games among the students, those that wanted to play, on most Saturdays. It would be fair to say that emotions could occasionally be highly charged during games and it was not unheard of for the occasional use of industrial language, if for example someone had been tacked rather heavily or the referee had given offside for what seemed to be a perfectly legitimate goal. Other recreational activities included amateur theatre for those who were that way inclined. Productions were put on once or twice a year, either a play or a Gilbert& Sullivan opera. I recall a fine rendition of H.M.S Pinafore one Christmas. These would take place in what was known as a "common room" which was a very large room where the community would go to after meals for recreation. There was no television, but there was a radio for those who wanted to listen to music or hear the cricket or tennis commentary. In addition, there was snooker and table tennis and there were also games available, monopoly and the like, for those that enjoyed those games. After all meals it was usual, weather permitting, for everyone to take a walk around the grounds, no doubt to work off the meal, and then they would go to the common room to talk or take part in any of the recreational activities. It was encouraged that individuals would not walk or recreate with particular friends, or go with the same people each day. The encouragement was that each person would be treated the same and that special friendships would not take place. It meant that after meals, brothers would leave the refectory and would pair up with whoever they met up with. This could be quite difficult and awkward, particularly if one met up with someone with whom they had absolutely nothing in common. This was what community living was all about and we had to try and make it work.

As the months passed by, I was finding that I was becoming more and more insular. Whilst I was still taking part in all the necessary activities and going through the motions of being a member of the community, I was spending a lot more time on my own and doing solitary things. I doubt that anyone had really been aware of this, because nobody was close enough to me, or anybody else, to even notice. In addition, it was part of the Redemptorist life to spend some time on one's own. However, for me, a naturally sociable person, I also found that being on my own was also very difficult and very lonely. I was definitely not built for a solitary life and I was forever questioning in my mind if I could reach my goal of becoming a priest, and if I did, would I be able to cope with a life that did not include a wife and a family.

Over the period of the summer months, I had noticed that I had developed an overall lack of appetite and increasing tiredness. Initially, I put this down to being uncertain about my future and having a degree of anxiety and stress. It could also have been caused by worry about my studies and forthcoming examinations. I was finding it difficult to keep pace with some of the others and to understand the lessons in these difficult subjects. Once more, my lack of being content and happy, was affecting my ability to study to the correct level and I found myself making excuses to do other tasks, and almost anything other than studying.

My lack of appetite and increasing nausea was beginning to show by now. I was six feet tall and naturally slim, and my weight rarely varied between eleven and eleven and a half stones. The food at Perth and Hawkstone, whilst plain, was also quite tasty and wholesome, so I was used to being a normal weight. Eventually, the nausea started to take an effect on me and I was unable to eat a normal healthy diet. Within a further month, I had lost over a stone in weight and it was beginning to show. From my normal slim build, I was starting to look decidedly gaunt and thin and it was more and more affecting my ability to do my normal daily activities. I had not told anybody that I was feeling ill. I did not feel close enough to tell anybody and I had not seen a doctor since my third year at Erdington some years earlier. Eventually, one of the Brothers noticed that I was not eating and that I was feeling unwell and he must have noticed my reticence in doing nothing about it. He therefore told my superior, Father Manson, who while he was not the most sympathetic of people; he told me I was looking ill and he insisted that I consulted the local doctor in Hodnet.

The resident General Practitioner at Hodnet examined me and told me that he thought I may have a stomach disorder, although he was unsure what it was, because it was unusual due to my relative youth. I was not too sure about this, because after six years of fried bread and beans for breakfast, for six days every week at Erdington, I had known that it was not the healthiest of diets. The doctor gave me medication and Father Manson instructed that I increased my food intake in order to try and put some weight back on. The normal breakfast at Hawkstone was cereals, coffee and rolls. Instead, he instructed the kitchen that I must have a full English fried breakfast every day of the week. I was feeling very self conscious about this every day, for while all my brothers had their simple breakfast, I was supposed to tuck into a giant portion of fried egg, bacon, sausage and all the usual trimmings while they watched on and could smell the aroma of the bacon. The plan backfired spectacularly, for instead of putting on weight and getting better, I became more nauseous and was sick after eating the fried breakfast. With hindsight, a fatty fried breakfast was hardly the right meal with someone having a stomach disorder. In the end, the breakfast was stopped and I was put on food supplements in order to keep up my weight. As I was feeling so unwell, I became more isolated and marginalised. I retired more and more to my room and did not take part in many of the daily activities. I was beginning to feel as if I was not really a part of the community any more and I whilst I was still there; I was on the outside looking in.

After many weeks of not getting any better, I was taken to consult a specialist who diagnosed that I had a duodenal ulcer. I was told that I would have to have an operation to rectify it. I had never been in Hospital before and I was nervous about what was going to happen. It was at times like this that I would have appreciated my family being around me. I needed the assurances and comfort that only your family can bring. As it was, I had no friends to confide in, and no-one to discuss any worries or fears that I might have had. One or two of the brothers did call to see me in my room and say that they hoped everything would be alright, but I must admit to feeling very much on my own and somewhat tentative of going into Hospital.

Father Manson himself took me into Shrewsbury Royal Infirmary early on the Monday morning, as planned. I just took a small bag with a few clothes, pyjamas and toothbrush. I was dressed in my conventional black suit, black shirt and white collar as worn by most clergy. It may have seemed overly formal, but that was how it was in those days. If I was not recognised as being something of a novelty before, then I was when I arrived at the Hospital. They had been expecting a clergyman, but not one so young. From the start I was treated cautiously and with respect, if not with a little apprehension. The Nursing staff referred to me as Reverend Nearey, and treated me initially as if they were walking on egg-shells. They knew that I had been brought in from the Catholic Seminary at Hawkstone Park and I think that they were perhaps more nervous about me than I was about them. They knew that it was a Monastery, but I am not sure what type of person and patient they were expecting to be dealing with.

After the first hour or two, the nurses began to realise that I was not an untouchable, a distant person that they had perhaps envisaged. I was just a twenty year old man who was extremely nervous and quite shy, particularly in the presence of women. They kept referring to me as Reverend, until I told them, quite nervously: *"I'm nobody special, just call me Steve."* After that they did call me Steve and it was a lot more relaxed. Even so, it was easy to get the impression that I was being viewed as something of an odyssey by everybody at the Hospital.

The following day I was due for my operation. I had been diagnosed as having a stomach ulcer. I had never been in hospital before and so I was naturally nervous. Since being admitted the previous day, I had not had any visitors from Hawkstone. It was at times like this that one would like to see a friendly face, before going under the knife, but there was nobody to confide in. It was a long way, some sixty miles or more, for my family to come and visit me, and none of them at that time had a car and public transport was not an easy option. I would have been grateful to see one or more of the brothers from Hawkstone, if only for some moral support, but nobody came that day. Fortunately, the Nurses were very good and very kind and they did their best to put me at ease before I went for my operation. I had been told by the specialist that my operation would be to repair the damage caused by an ulcer. I had no idea what this entailed, and so I just put my trust in them, relaxed and hoped for the best.

Around late morning I was taken on my bed and up to the theatre for my operation. Before I knew it I was back again, in my bed on the ward, and a nurse was calling my name in my sub-conscious. Drowsily, I regained consciousness. I could not really speak, I just felt so bad and the pain was terrible. The operation had taken well over three hours and the anaesthetic made me feel very sleepy and not wanting to communicate. The Nurses kept checking on me quite frequently. I told them that I felt terrible, but they told me that it was normal. I had never had an operation before, and so I did not know quite what to expect. All I did know was that I was in awful pain and I was feeling very, very sickly. By late afternoon, [I knew it was late, as it was dark outside and the ward lights were on]. I started to feel nauseas and suddenly and without warning, I violently vomited up bright red blood. This happened with increasing regularity during the evening and I was given replacement blood and was under constant observation by Doctors and Nurses. I knew instinctively that something had gone very wrong with the operation. The anxiety on the faces of the Nurses and Doctors told a similar story. Yet still, nobody had come to see me and I was feeling very alone. Despite feeling confident and cared for by the medical staff, I still had not had a visit from anybody from Hawkstone or from home and I was feeling quite isolated and alone. By late evening, most of the other patients were in bed and had gone to sleep. It was now dark and late at night. I was still vomiting fresh red blood and feeling much, much worse. A doctor came to visit me at my bedside and told me that I may have to go back to the operating theatre and have another operation. They were waiting for the surgeon to come back to the hospital before they would decide.

I waited and waited for what seemed an eternity and nothing seemed to be happening. But then suddenly, the curtains from around my bed opened and there was Father Manson from Hawkstone. Whilst it was good to see somebody I recognised, and he was kind and of course concerned, he was in no way close to me, in the way that a family member or even a friend would be. He had been called out by the Hospital during the night because my condition had deteriorated and he came to the Hospital to administer the Last Rights to me. In the Catholic Church, one of the sacraments, like communion, are the Last Rights, and it was usually given to people who were dying. It is nowadays also given to people who are ill, and to ask God for a recovery, but at the time, it was usually administered to Catholics who were in danger of death.

It was really traumatic then, at the young age of twenty one years old, and until recently in good health, to be facing death so young. I lay there listening to the prayers from Father Manson and I was silently praying to God myself, that I would come through this operation, so that I could go on and live my life and also become his priest.

One of the nurses, Margaret, was particularly kind and very reassuring. She told me that my parents had been called and that they were on the way to see me straight away. Whilst that was very reassuring, in that I was desperate to see them, I was also extremely anxious that they had been called during the night. This made me really fearful that my condition was extremely serious.

Then at around 2 a.m. in the morning, the specialist came to me and told me that I was going to the operating theatre straight away, as there had been a bleed in my stomach since my operation, and that it had to be stemmed. To say that I was anxious was a huge understatement. My nurse, Margaret, came with me by my bedside and held my hand. I was shaking and very nervous. The journey on the trolley through the dimly lit corridors and then into the lift, seemed to take an age. Eventually, we reached the operating theatre which was flooded with bright lights. I felt so ill that I almost did not care, and I just let them get on with whatever they had to do. I remember looking up at the anaesthetist as he gave me an injection into my hand and my last memory as I tried in vain to count to ten, was whether I would wake up again, or was this to be the end?

The next thing that I remember was sensing daylight, and I opened my eyes. I think, to my surprise, I was back in my bed and on the ward. It must have been mid morning as there were nurses buzzing around and making beds and treating other patients on the ward. A nurse came up-to me and with a big beaming smile said: *"Well, you're back then, its good to see you"!* She was a tall black nurse from Ghana, and she was full of the joys of spring. Immediately it made me feel better to see her smiling face. *"You've got visitors"* she said with a huge smile. I glance around and there, walking through the double doors of the ward were my parents. I had never been so pleased to see them in my entire life. Until that point I had felt that I was completely on my own. I had never realised just how much I had missed my Mum and Dad, even though for the past three years they had only played an occasional part in my life. My time at Hawkstone seemed to have taken over that role and I was then a part of the Redemptorist family and community, rather than a member my own family. I was very tired and very weak at that point, but I was quietly happy and content seeing Mum and Dad once more, when in walked Father Manson who was my Student Master from Hawkstone and one of the Brothers. I should have been pleased to see them. They had been good to me and they were very concerned for my well being. Mum and Dad were sat on one side of my bed, and Father Manson and the brother sat on the other. I felt a strange contradiction. At that point, I just wanted my parents but instead I had my real family and then my adopted family, [the Redemptorists], on the other. It felt as if they were vying for my attention, the two parts of my life that I had been battling with for so many years. Mum and Dad had booked into a Guest House in Shrewsbury so that they could visit me again the following day before going home the day afterwards. I was looking forward to seeing them again as I managed to see them so in frequently. It had been almost two years since I had last been with them just before my move from Perth to Hawkstone Hall.

In the evening after my second operation, the specialist came in to see me. He was accompanied by another junior doctor and Margaret, my special care nurse. He examined me and checked my wounds, and then he said: *"Stephen, you gave us all something of a scare last night, but you should be alright soon!"* He looked and sounded extremely relieved, and pleased that I seemed to be on the mend. There was no recurrence of the haemorrhage. He did not expand on exactly what had happened late that night, and I did not want to delve into it too deeply. I was just happy to be there, still alive, and hopefully, back on the road to recovery. I did however ask him if he had cured the stomach ulcer and he replied to me that it had turned out not to be a stomach ulcer after all. He told me that they had found a rare congenital abnormality of my duodenum and that it had now been dealt with. I did not feel inclined to discuss the details of this any further.

Having had two operations within two days, and two lots of anaesthetic, I was feeling extremely tired and weak. I had also lost a lot of weight before I was admitted to Hospital, and so my recovery period was not going to be a speedy one. My parents kept visiting me, as did different members of the community at Hawkstone. In my head, I still had this ongoing battle as to exactly where I belonged. For the first few days after my operation I saw my parents and several members of my family at visiting times. This only served to strengthen the bond between us and it gave me a hankering to want to go back home with them and not to return immediately to Hawkstone. I also had visits from Fr. Manson and several of the brothers, some of whom were my friends from Perth and Erdington. It seemed to me that I was in a tug of war, if only in my head and that I was in the middle, being tugged at by both parties. I knew that if I had been forced to make a decision at that moment in time, I would have left the Seminary at Hawkstone and gone back to live a new life back at home with my family. Perhaps this was an emotional response made purely because of my illness. Perhaps once I was fully recovered and feeling well enough, I would just return to Hawkstone and continue my chosen way of life.

Visiting times occupied just a very small portion of each day, and there were many hours to fill during the rest of the time. My progress was slow because I had lost so much weight, blood and had had two serious operations. I had been in hospital for over a week and I was beginning to feel institutionalised, just as I had been at Hawkstone, Perth and Erdington. Of course, it was a completely different type of institutionalisation. As a patient I just slotted into the routine of each day like everybody else. Because of the drama and the frequent visits by priests and brothers from Hawkstone, I became a bit of an oddity on the ward. It seemed that the ward was always full of clergymen. The nurses still seemed to treat me differently to the other patients, even though I tried my hardest to join in and be the same as the others. The nurses knew that I was from the Seminary and that I was training to be a priest and they were somehow different with me. I was not sure if it was just out of respect for what I was, or if it was to do with the mystique that went along with the life I was living at Hawkstone. I suppose that my natural reserve contributed to the way people responded to me. My life for the past few years had always been about remaining quiet, reserved and keeping to myself. I was polite, softly spoken and not demanding in any way, so I was an easy patient to deal with in that respect. I just let them get on with it and was quite passive, yet I could understand why the staff would keep a nervous distance.

The one nurse who just treated me exactly like the other patients was Yolande, the girl from Ghana. She was a terrific nurse and was always so full of fun. She was happy at her work and would smile and laugh all the time. She treated me just the same as all the other patients. She would take all the embarrassment out of "bed baths" and similar personal treatments, by laughing her way through it. She made me feel so much better each day just because of her sunny disposition and the way she did her work.

There was another nurse who I could relate to very easily. I would always refer to all the nurses as "Nurse", but she insisted that I called her Margaret. She was young, about the same age as me, and very pretty with long dark hair, tied up. She had accompanied me to the operating theatre that night and held my hand, giving me reassurance, at a time when I felt very ill and extremely scared. She was also the first nurse I had set eyes upon when I came around after my operation. At that time, I was feeling quite alone without my family, and yet she gave me that calming influence and reassurance that I needed. Whereas I would "pass the time of day" with all the other staff I could really talk to Margaret. We seemed to be on the same wave length and had something in common that it was hard to grasp. Whenever Margaret had time during her busy work day, she would come and ask me how I was feeling and have a chat while doing my treatments. In the afternoons after visiting time, it was a quiet period on the ward. Usually I would have a sleep, but if it was quiet Margaret would come and talk with me. Initially, it was just chit chat and then banter, but as the days passed by we began to talk more in depth. She asked me about my life at the Seminary and I would ask her all about being a nurse, which I found to be fascinating. At Perth and Hawkstone I would never open up and talk to anybody about my innermost feelings and yet within a few short days I had told her, effectively a stranger, more about my life than I had ever told to another person. I suppose that being in Hospital in a vulnerable condition, I had allowed my defences to come down, and I spoke more freely. I did not however let her know at that stage that I was either undecided or unhappy with my life. I told her that when I had recovered I would return to Hawkstone to convalesce or perhaps that I would be sent to one of the other monasteries in the countryside, away from the pressures of study, so that I could return to full health. Margaret was very open about her life too. She was hoping to be promoted to Staff Nurse very soon and she loved her career as a nurse. She was just perfect for the job. She was bright, intelligent witty, but above all she was a really caring person and an ideal nurse. She was not married but she had had a regular boyfriend called Dave but they had recently broken up and gone down their separate ways.

A couple of days passed by, but I was not very much nearer to being discharged from Hospital. I kept getting infections in the long wound in my stomach where I had been opened up twice, and the stitches also became infected. After a lengthy and traumatic stay at Shrewsbury Hospital, it would have been natural to want to get out as soon as possible. But I did not have the motivation to want to go back to Hawkstone to recuperate. Strangely, I felt more comfortable and at ease where I was in Hospital. It was like being in a safe haven, I did not have to make any decisions and I was content to stay there for the time being and just recover without the pressures of normal life

My nurse, Yolanda was back on duty after a couple of days off and she was great at keeping the patients cheerful. She was so friendly and happy and I knew that she had taken a liking to me. She too would stop and talk whenever she got an opportunity during treatment or when the ward was quiet. Margaret was off duty for a couple of days break and I missed her. I had forged something of a connection with her and I missed our little chats very much. I was looking forward to seeing her back on duty and on the ward again soon. I had never had anybody to confide in and being able to talk personally and confide in her, was a great comfort to me and it made me feel good.

In the meantime, my parents and family kept visiting me regularly despite the long journey back and to, from Cheshire. My Mum was asking me if I thought I may be allowed home to convalesce. I told her that I thought it would be unlikely, but that I would speak with Father Manson the next time he visited. For the first time ever, I was beginning to conclude that I did not want to return to Hawkstone, at least until I was fully recovered. It was becoming clear in my mind that despite my illness being caused by a congenital defect, that part of the reason for my illness, was my life at the Seminary. I felt that I needed a complete break so that I could clear my mind, and be able to come to my decision from a neutral point of view and without the unintentional pressures that I would be under should I return to Hawkstone to recuperate.

All of this was going through my head as I lay in my hospital bed. Yet I knew that once I would speak to other people, my mind could quite easily be swayed one way or another. Whilst I knew that my new home was then Hawkstone, I also thought that it would do me good to go back to my parent's home for a period of time to regain my strength before returning. I spoke to Father Manson the next time he visited me. He was of the old school and was the type of person who would retain a stiff upper lip and just get on with things. I thought that he would expect me to do the same and that I should return to Hawkstone or go to another of the Redemptorists residences in the peace and quiet of the countryside to re-cooperate.

When I spoke to him, he told me that my parent's home was no longer where I lived and that I should return to Hawkstone where I would be excused studies for several weeks until I was fully recovered. He did though offer as a possible alternative, to send me to another of the Redemptorist Houses in a rural part of the countryside, which would be beneficial in helping me back to full health. However, I replied that I would not know anybody at any of the other houses and would feel quite isolated and alone. I said that I would prefer to return to Hawkstone, if I was not permitted to go home to my parents. At this, Father Manson seemed to sense my huge disappointment and given my poor state of health he agreed, against his better judgement, that I could return to my parent's home, for a short period of time, in order to convalesce, once I was discharged from the hospital.

I believe that Father Manson had already sensed my uncertainty about my future and that by allowing me to go home, I would be subjected to all manner of influences that would not have been beneficial to my continuing with the Redemptorist Order. That may well have been the outcome, however, I needed to find out for myself, what my future was going to be, and it was only by being aware of all my alternatives, that I would ever be able to make a definite decision. As I slowly began to feel stronger I was beginning to feel a little more relaxed and at peace with myself. At long last, I felt that I was in a neutral territory, a safe haven and that I was the only person that would be able to decide in which direction I would travel next.

The next day I was pleased to see Margaret back on duty. When I saw her walk onto the ward it lifted my spirits enormously. I don't know what it was about her, but she made me feel good, just to have her around. When she came to me to change my dressings, and to do the regular checks, she said: *"I'm glad you're still here, Steve", I thought you may have been discharged over the weekend."* She quickly realised what she had said and then quickly corrected herself. *"I didn't mean I want you to stay in Hospital any longer, I just meant that I wanted to see you before you have to go!"* I smiled: *"No, I'm really pleased to see you too"* I said picking my words carefully. *"I've missed having you around the ward".* That was something of an understatement on my part. The truth was, that I had feelings for this nurse, this girl, that I had never experienced before. It was surreal. There we were, she my nurse, and me her patient, and we had both just said a lot more than the words we had just spoken. There was a lot more feeling expressed than the words that had been used, and we both knew it. She had to move onto the next patient, as it was the busy morning period on the Ward. Afterwards I lay quietly in my bed just pondering the possible meaning of the exchange we had just had. I had no idea, if it could possibly mean anything. Here I was, totally confused about who I was and where I was going and now I had genuine feelings for my nurse. It felt as if I was in a war zone and somebody had just tossed a hand grenade into the middle of it all! All I knew for certain was that I was experiencing feelings for Margaret that I had never sought, but was like nothing I had ever experienced during my sheltered life. It was yet another complication in an already complicated life and I really did not know in which direction I was going to turn.

Over the next couple of days I talked to Margaret much more. She told me about herself and her life, and the more she told me, the more convinced I was that she was a lovely person. Within a matter of days, I felt as if I knew her really well and it felt really good. I spoke to her quite openly about my life at Hawkstone and before that. She was fascinated by it all. I was open, but I was also guarded on some topics. She found it very hard to comprehend the life of celibacy that I had recently committed to, and rather unconvincingly, I tried to explain the right reasons for it. I have always been an open book, and during our conversations she must have realised that I was very uncertain about my future and that I had doubts about whether I would continue on, to finally become a priest. I told Margaret that I was planning to go home to my parents to convalesce after I had been discharged, instead of going back to Hawkstone. She said that she thought it would be a good idea on medical grounds, but she seemed really happy at this and said that maybe we could see each other again. I told her that I hoped that we could, but secretly, I could not imagine not seeing Margaret again. She had taken over my thoughts and all I could do was think about her all of the time. I had absolutely no idea where all of this would lead. All I could do was to take every day as it came along and to see what happened next. At last the day finally arrived. My surgeon came to see me along with the ward Sister and Margaret, and told me that I had been making good progress and that I would be discharged the following day. I said: *"Oh, that's great!"* But I did not mean it. It was the strangest of feelings! Why would I not want to leave Hospital? Yet when he said those words, I felt totally insecure once more. The Men's Surgical Ward at Shrewsbury Royal Infirmary had become a safe harbour for me, a place where I had no pressure, where all the problems in my life had been swept away for a few short weeks. The next day I would need to start facing all those demons yet again, only this time I had one new complication. It was Margaret. Meeting her had highlighted just how much I was missing family life and how difficult it was to live a solitary life.

The next day, I awoke and immediately I sensed that it was the start of something new in my life. I was not sure what it was to be, but I had a feeling that nothing would be quite the same again for very long. After all the final routine hospital checks, I changed into my outdoor clothing and waited on the ward to be collected. Margaret had already been to see me and I gave her my home telephone number. Likewise, she gave me her number and her address. I had become very fond of several of the staff, particularly Yolanda and the Ward Sister, but it was especially Margaret, that I was going to miss the most.

At 11am, one of the brothers from Hawkstone arrived on the ward to collect me, and take me back to the seminary, before driving me back home to my parents. While he waited, I said my goodbye's to all the medical staff that had looked after me so well. I found it a wrench to leave and saying goodbye was very emotional. I gave each of the staff a polite kiss on the cheek and a hug. Finally I said goodbye to Margaret in the same way, but with a kiss and a hug that said something completely different, but without using any actual words. As I walked away to the car with Brother John, I glanced back to Margaret and the nurses who were waving, and I just wondered whether I was destined to ever see her once again?

On the journey back to Hawkstone I chatted with Brother John about my stay in hospital and what had been happening at the seminary since I had been away. I had been in Hospital for over four weeks. As we talked I spoke the words, but my mind was somewhere completely different. Father Manson had arranged for me to stay overnight at Hawkstone before I would be taken to convalesce at my parent's home in Marple, Cheshire. Father Manson clearly wanted me to remember that my home was at Hawkstone. When we got back, he came to see me and welcomed me home, but he made it very clear to me that he expected me back at the seminary once I was feeling better again. Although I said all the right things to him, my mind was a thousand miles away and I was in no condition to contemplate long term commitments to anybody or anything at that particular moment in time.

The following day Brother John drove me back to Marple. I could not get there quickly enough. I just needed time and space to sort out my muddled mind. The journey back was like a journey of re-discovery. I had not been back to my parent's home for well over two years and I was excited about it. Brother John wished me a speedy recovery and told me to enjoy a few weeks rest and that he would see me then. When I arrived home, Mum and Dad and my younger brother Mike were there to welcome me home. Even my old bed in the back bedroom was still there, just as I had left it, with the picture of my beloved Manchester City in pride of place above the head of the bed. It was good just to do nothing for a while. Everything at Hawkstone had been so regimented and what with Mum's home made cooking I soon started to regain my appetite and started to feel a little more like my old self. It was most unusual just to take each day as it came, without an agenda, and to do whatever I wanted to each day. For a couple of days, I just did nothing and enjoyed the peace and the space, but then I started to become restless, and started thinking about all the key things going on in my life. My short stay at home was just a port in a storm, a safe haven in choppy waters. It was not a permanent resting place, or was it? I started thinking again about Hawkstone. After all, I was only on loan to my parents and I was expected back there within a few short weeks to resume the journey I had started. Would I go back? How would I cope? In my mind, I had a strong feeling that if I ever went back to Hawkstone, it would be for good and I would never leave again. My parents, although delighted to have me back home and to take care of me, had no idea of the inner turmoil I was in, and to them, being home was just a short holiday, a place to rest and recuperate until I was strong enough to return and continue my journey to becoming a priest. My elder brother, Arthur was well on his way to being ordained a parish priest, and I knew that it was what my parents wanted for me too. It was an honour and a privilege for Catholic parents to have a son become a priest, and two would have been even more so.

The following day, I had a phone call from Father Manson, checking to see how I was progressing, and passing on the good wishes of all my brothers at the seminary. He didn't push me to say when I would be returning, and I did not give him any inclination as to when that would be. I had been at home for five days, and the novelty was beginning to wear off. I knew that this was just a temporary stopping off place, and so I was unable to feel settled, because I knew that a major decision had to made, and quite soon. The fact that I was still some way off being returned to full health, did not help my decision making. Then, that same evening, something happened that was to make matters became even more complicated than they had ever been before.

When I had left the hospital some six days earlier, I had experienced a totally new feeling in my life. It was a feeling that was all encompassing and too strong for me to ignore. This was not supposed to have happened. I had taken a vow of chastity just two years earlier. I had developed strong feelings for a girl, not just any girl, but my nurse at the hospital. During my last week there, she had been constantly on my mind and Margaret became the focus of all my thoughts and attentions. It was not something that I had wanted to happen, or had even encouraged, but it had happened, and I did not know how to deal with this new situation. When we had parted at the hospital, I just knew that it was not a final goodbye. Yet since I had returned home, I had done nothing about it, because I did not know how to deal with this new situation. Margaret had been in my thoughts every single day since we had waved goodbye, but I was now sixty miles away, I did not have a car, and I did not know how to drive. Our paths had parted, had gone in different directions and I did not know how to get them back together and even if I could, where it would all lead to?

That same evening that I had spoken to Father Manson, I had a phone call from Shrewsbury. *"Steve, I have to talk to you!"* she said: I knew straight away that it was Margaret and I was shocked, but absolutely delighted at the same time. *"I've been out of my mind, going crazy"* she continued. *"I just can't stop thinking about you. I had to phone you and see how you are."* I replied: *"I am fine"* I stumbled: *"I am just so happy to hear from you. I've wanted to call you and speak, but everything has become so complicated and I just didn't know how to deal with things, I still don't."* I replied: *"I really need to speak with you properly and try to sort matters out".*

Margaret told me that she had to see me and said that she would come to Marple. I said that I was desperate to see her and that we had to speak. There was something special between us that meant that we had to deal with it, but I had no idea how I could do it. Surely it was all too complicated? I suggested that it was not a good idea for her to come here, as we needed to be alone. I had a little money that I had saved up in a post office account from being at school. It was made up of gifts from various people and pocket money that Mum had sent to me every week. I had no other money of my own, as we did not use money at Hawkstone, so I went to the Post Office and withdrew what I needed. I told Margaret that I would get the train to Shrewsbury and meet her at the train station the next day. I took the train to Manchester and then the connection to Shrewsbury. I was lost and pensive as I sat on the train, wondering what would happen, what we would say, and where it would all end. My stay in Hospital had thrown up yet another complication, another option, another possible direction for me to go.

As the train pulled into the platform I walked towards the ticket office where we had arranged to meet. At first I did not recognise her! I had only ever seen her in her blue nurse's uniform and cap. Would she recognise me? She had only really seen me in pyjamas and dressing gown, and here I was in a dark suit and pristine white shirt with no tie, smart but perhaps a touch too formal, but it was all I had. Among a group of people at the ticket office I saw her waving and smiling, and quickly went straight towards her. She was in a bright yellow dress covered by an open raincoat, as it had been raining hard. I followed my natural inclination which was to put my arms around her and give her a kiss on the cheek. She responded and it felt good and it felt natural. Perhaps for the first time in my life, I was following my natural inclinations rather than what my head told me I should do. We held hands as we walked out of the station where we stopped. I had no idea what to do or where to go next. *"Where shall we go?"* I asked: *"Its up-to you"* she smiled. *"Well, I don't know Shrewsbury at all, I've lived in a monastery here for two years and I have never been into the town!"* I replied. At this she was a little shocked: Of course, she would not have thought about that. Why would she? At that point I realised that she knew absolutely nothing about me, other than the chats we had held in hospital, and I knew even less about Margaret. The only thing that we had in common at that stage was a strong and emotional attraction, but it was a very good place to start. I had heard of love at first sight, and perhaps this was it.

As it was raining I suggested that we went to the cinema. *"Gone with the Wind"* was showing at the Apollo and although it was a 1937 film, it seemed absolutely appropriate at the time. I must have been pretty awkward in this type of situation. I had never really taken a girl out before and I must have been all fingers and thumbs. Just about everything I said and did was clumsy and it showed. I think that Margaret had got the impression that I was pretty inexperienced in the dating game, but it did not seem to matter. We were wrapped up in one another and despite all the probable hurdles and obstacles to us being together, we just carried on as if nothing else mattered. To me, Margaret was the first real woman that I had encountered. I did not mean to feel the way I was feeling about her. I had met other women, although not many and I had met other nurses, but none of them had any affect on me at all, in the way that I had feelings for her. To Margaret, I must have seemed like an unattainable target, someone not to be touched. Not only was I young and inexperienced, but I was shy, nervous, awkward and clumsy in everything I said and did. I had no idea whatsoever why I would be attractive to her. I had lived in a boy's only school for six years, in a monastery in Scotland for a year, and now I was a student priest in a seminary, just a few miles down the road. Not only that, I had recently taken a vow of chastity just three years before. In plain speaking, that meant that in terms of physical and emotional relationships, women were not meant to play any part in my life. So why would I be attractive to Margaret? I did not know, but I had to ask her. I needed to know the reason why.

It was perhaps not too difficult to understand why I was so struck by Margaret. She was my nurse; she had cared for me when I felt at my most vulnerable. She understood me and she talked to me in private, at a time when I was very down, lonely and extremely ill. In addition, she was very beautiful. Perhaps if we had met in entirely different circumstances, the attraction may never have happened. Yet it had, and somehow, sometime soon, we had to resolve what, if anything was going to happen next. This was a critical moment in time, and nothing was going to stop it from happening, but the day of reckoning was around the corner and at some point soon, it would have to be reckoned with, and crucial decisions needed making. But that day was for another time. We sat in the Station Buffet Bar, not the most romantic of places for a first date, but to us it really did not matter. We held hands and looked into each other's eyes over our coffee. We did not speak a lot, because what we felt for each other on that day, just said it all. Words were just not necessary.

We glanced up at the large station clock. It was seven O'clock in the evening and my train was on the platform. I had to go home again that evening, yet I felt that I had only just arrived as the time had passed so quickly. I had told everybody that I was just going for a day out in order to obtain some peace and tranquillity. After all, I was still unwell and needed rest and recuperation. As Margaret left me at the train door, we kissed, then held each other and we promised to see each other again soon in Stockport. There was still unfinished business between us.

Back at home the next day, I was talking with my parents about Hawkstone. Mum and Dad seemed keen to know all about my life there and wanted to discuss my future plans. I avoided the subject as much as I could. The time was not right. We spoke about everything except going back to the seminary. I told them that I did not feel fit enough yet to think about returning there. They perhaps thought it was unusual that I did not speak much about Hawkstone and my life there, and that I was not making any plans to return. If anything, I was trying to avoid the subject and when they spoke about it, I would change the subject and move onto something entirely different. My mind was in too much of a muddle to want to talk about my future plans and what may or not happen. Father Manson would call quite regularly and enquire as to how I was progressing. I did not want to be drawn into discussing a date for my return. There were now too many complications and I did not know how I was ever going to reach a decision. I just told him that I did not feel well enough to return yet and that I would let him know as soon as I felt able. He seemed to know that all was not well. In the meantime, if I had been unsure about myself before I met Margaret, then I was now doubly so. It was not like making a decision to go out for a day. Whatever I decided was going to be life changing and probably forever. I had arranged with Margaret to meet her again locally in Stockport and I had arranged to meet her at the Railway Station. I was so looking forward to seeing her again, and I know that she felt the same way too. There was a connection between us that was getting stronger and stronger. When I got to Stockport Station her train was twenty minutes late, so I went into the station buffet bar and ordered a coffee while I waited. As I sat there cradling a mug of coffee in my hands, I began to wonder just where it was all leading. I did not want to face the facts, but I could only see problems ahead. Somehow, it seemed that the timing was all wrong and I just wished that we had met at another time, perhaps another place and in different circumstances. As I mused over the last dregs of my coffee, I saw her train pull onto the platform. It reminded me perfectly of that famous 1945 movie "Brief Encounters". Surely our relationship was not going to finish in the same way? I met her at the carriage, and suddenly, all worries and fears disappeared, albeit momentarily. The only thing on my mind was that we were together again. We talked happily and about nothing in particular. She was telling me all about what was happening at Shrewsbury Royal Infirmary and I told her all about my family, and my time at home. It was as if we both knew that there were big issues to be sorted out, but not just yet. We wanted to put them to one side and pretend that they did not exist. For the moment, we just wanted to enjoy the time we had together. There would be another time to discuss the problems that lay ahead for us.

We spent the day together doing nothing particularly exciting. We went for some lunch and then had a walk around the shops, followed by a lovely stroll in the park. It was a beautiful day and it was just so relaxing walking among the trees and along the winding stream. It was enough just to be in each other's company and there was no need for grand gestures or to go to extravagant places.

As the day began to draw to a close, we began to speak about some of our frustrations. We both wished that we were not living so far apart and that we could see each other more frequently. The distance itself, some sixty miles or so, was not really the issue. Margaret had a car and it was just over an hour's journey to Marple. During our discussions at the hospital we had discussed life at Hawkstone. She was aware of my being unsettled there and that I did not know if I could cope with the solitary lifestyle that the future offered me. Perhaps our meeting was the catalyst for me making the decision to finally make the break. At that moment, I found myself unable to say definitely that I would leave, and Margaret was not going to ask me to do so. I knew from little comments that she had already made, that she did not want to be the sole reason for me leaving Hawkstone for good. We walked back to the station that evening and despite the fact that we had spent a lovely day together, we both knew that we could not continue too much longer as we were. There were major problems to be overcome, if indeed we wanted to be together. Margaret was still on the rebound from a steady relationship, and I was effectively spoken for, not to another woman, [she could cope with that], but to the Catholic Church. That was a sizable obstacle to overcome and not to be taken lightly. We both had thinking to do.

Back at home I was still living in "no man's land", it was a safe place to be for the time being, but time was running out. Mum, Dad, and my family were asking me awkward questions, and I was unable to give them satisfactory answers. Father Manson was asking me when I would feel ready to return to the Monastery. I still could not give him an answer. Then of course, there was Margaret! So far, Margaret, like me, was being swept along on a sea of emotion, and calm reasoning had not come into the equation, but the day of reckoning would not be long in coming. We both knew it and we were both afraid of it.

Over the next few days I spoke at length to Margaret and was more and more open with her. We spoke for a long time by telephone without ever reaching a satisfactory conclusion. I had already told her, that before being admitted to hospital, that I had strong misgivings about remaining at Hawkstone. I let her know that part of the reason for me being in hospital may have been due to the stress and anxiety of living in the seminary and then there was perhaps the most telling admission of them all: *"Margaret"*, I said, with great emotion in my voice: *"Meeting you, and feeling as I do about you, has finally made me realise that I don't want to stay at Hawkstone. I want to leave and be with you"*. I had hoped and thought that this was what she would want to hear, but I was wrong to believe that she would be able to cope with the news I had just broken to her. It was too much for her to deal with. There was no doubt that she still felt the same about me, and she told me so, but there was a sad feeling of resignation in her voice as she spoke to me. *"Steve,"* she said *"I **cannot** be the reason for you not becoming a priest. I could never live with the knowledge of that"*.

Two or three more days passed by. I was still at home and I was starting to feel better, at least physically. I was eating well and going out for long walks, mostly on my own, but sometimes with my brother, and it was good to spend time with my parents. However, inside of me, I was in turmoil. I had not heard from Margaret for a few days. She told me that she was on a training course away from home and that she would call me on her return. I felt that I was perhaps losing her due to my indecision. That evening I went on a long walk on my own. I just had to decide and then do something about it. I must have walked for I don't know how many miles into the countryside, musing over the options. There were so many pros and cons to consider, and then there was Margaret! Eventually, the decision just came into my head: I was going to leave Hawkstone, no matter what else happened. I held that thought in my mind as I walked home that night, and I was going to keep it, irrespective of what would happen with Margaret. That night I did not sleep well, if at all, but my decision was finally made. I just had to decide how I was going to finally make the break. The next morning I woke up, and my mindset was just the same. I felt nervous and tentative. I was going to telephone Fr. Manson and break the news to him that I was not going to return. My mind was finally made up. I made sure that I was on my own at the time. My brother had gone to work and my parents were both out. I picked up the telephone and called the Redemptorists and asked to speak with Father Manson. The brother who answered the phone asked me who I was and then asked me to wait while he located Fr.Manson. It must have been minutes before he arrived and in the meantime I went through what I was going to say to him, over and over in my mind! Eventually the phoned was picked up and Father Manson answered in his usual stern voice: *"Good Morning Brother Nearey, how are you today?"* With my voice trembling with emotion I blurted out: *"Fine Father, but I've decided that I want to leave Hawkstone and I don't want to come back!"* I had not said any of the things I had wanted to and practiced, and had not offered him any explanation of any kind. The line went quiet for what seemed like an age. Then, in his normal cool and calm manner he said: *"Well, it's not as simple as that is it?"* He continued in his calm and controlled manner: *"You've been very ill and you were unsettled before you went into Hospital. You can't make a decision like this without coming back here so that we can talk about it."* His manner was very authoritative. My reply by comparison was stumbling and nervous: *"No, I really don't want to come back. My mind is made up"* But I did not feel or sound decisive in what I had just said. Father Manson continued: *"I will send Brother John to collect you on Monday; we really must deal with this matter in a proper manner. We will talk about it after the weekend, when you come back".* Meekly I accepted his authority and I agreed, and although I could quite easily have not returned again, I knew deep down, that it was the right way to do things. After I put the phone down I felt crest-fallen. Our telephone conversation had not worked out how I had planned it, and now I felt that I was back at first base. It had been several weeks since I had left the seminary to go into hospital and then go back home to recover. Now the thought of going back into Hawkstone and the structured, rigid way of life, seemed suddenly alien to me. Up-to this point, all my feelings were about the rights or wrongs of the seminary life and whether it was right for me or not. At least I felt that I had made a decision based on that, and not about meeting Margaret and the relationship that had now developed between us.

The next day, I was beginning to get my head together a little, and I was reconciled to the fact that I was going back to Hawkstone, if only for a short while until I had sorted matters out. In my mind, I had already decided that I would go back there, have discussions with Fr. Manson and then confirm my decision to leave and to start a new life, whatever that might entail. At this point I had not discussed any of this with my family, although I had primed them that I was feeling unsettled there, so that it would not come as too much of a shock when I finally made the break. I knew that I was going to find it a great harder to break the news to my parents than to my adopted family at Hawkstone. They had been so proud of the fact that I was going to be a Redemptorist and a priest. The next day, Saturday, I was to get shock news that would turn my world upside down yet again. The postman arrived with a letter addressed simply to *"Steve Nearey,"* at my family home. I opened it eagerly with a knife, as I could see the neat round slanted hand-writing that was Margaret's trade mark. I had not spoken to her for several days, due to her training course and I was excited to read what she had to say. I had so much wanted to tell her my news, and to tell her that I had made the decision to leave, that it had no bearing on how I felt about her. I needed her to know that. Eagerly I glanced at her letter: It read:

"My Dearest Darling Steve,

I have missed you so much since we last met. I have not spoken to you for a few days because I have been in so much turmoil that I have barely been able to work, eat or sleep. You have been constantly on my mind. But as much as I want you, I cannot have you, knowing that you are going to leave the monastery for me. I cannot bear the guilt and burden of feeling responsible for you not becoming a priest. That is just too much for me to cope with. I just feel that maybe we were not meant to be. You will make a wonderful Priest and I will always love you anyway. I cannot see you again Steve, it would be too painful to see what I have lost and I may always live to regret it, but I feel it will be for the best. I will never forget you Steve. Please try to forgive me for breaking your heart. You will always be in my thoughts." Margaret XX.

The letter was short and to the point. I gazed at it in stunned bewilderment for some minutes, trying to take in the enormity of it all. What cruel fate could arrange for me to take the biggest decision of my life, at exactly the same time that Margaret had decided to finish our relationship? Somehow, I knew it was the end for us. I had wanted to tell her that I was going to go back to the Seminary and that I would be coming out again. I had hoped that she would have waited for me, but I knew it was not to be and that it would have been unfair to ask her to do so.

I thought that I should try to phone her right away, and that maybe there would still be time to sort it all out. But how could I tell her that I was going back to Hawkstone when I did not know if or when I would leave again? It was impossible! I decided that the only course of action was to write. I told her in my letter that I was returning there in order to sort out my future one way or another. I let her know that I wanted to leave, but I could only do so by going back first of all, in order to do things properly and by the book. I told her that I loved her very much, but that I did not want to put her under any pressure or hurt her any more. Finally, I said to her that I wanted to be with her, but only if and when I had decided to leave for all the right reasons and when I was free to join her. I knew that the stakes were high and that the odds were stacked against me, but that was the only way to do it. I signed the letter, posted it to Margaret and then just hoped! On Monday morning I awoke and immediately felt that my entire life was about to change yet again. For the past six weeks I had experienced a whole new chapter in my life. Albeit due to unusual circumstances, my illness, I had experienced family life once more and a freedom of schedule that I had not been used to for over ten years. It had been a new experience to awake in the morning and not to be ruled by a bell that controlled just about every hour of my life. It may be too strong an expression to use to describe how I felt at that time, but a "return to jail" came into my mind. My brief relationship with Margaret had come to an end and I was heading back to the rigid lifestyle of the seminary. Once again I packed my small number of clothes and belongings and awaited the car to take me back to Shrewsbury. Mum and Dad also seemed sad that I would be leaving but they had grown used to me living away from home since I was eleven years old. They had no idea at this point, exactly how unsettled I was and how unsure I was, that I would be able to continue at Hawkstone. Brother John duly arrived mid morning. I said my farewells to my parents but this time I said: *"Look forward to seeing you again soon"*. It was an open statement, and they did not read too much into it, but it was the thought I had in my mind. I did not really know what was going to happen over the coming weeks and months. The journey back to Shropshire was a solemn one. I did not feel like I was returning to my home. I felt that I was going there for the first time. The short six weeks since I had left there, felt more like a year and instead of returning to a familiar place, I felt as if I was a visiting stranger, someone from the outside. Brother John was his normal and chirpy self on the journey. He was chatty and friendly and telling me all the news that had happened since I was last there. He asked me if I was pleased to be coming back home. To him, Hawkstone was home! He had been with the Redemptorists for nigh on forty years and he neither knew nor remembered any other place as home anymore. In answer to his question I replied: *"Yes, I am feeling better thanks, and I am looking forward to seeing everyone again"*. I worded my response carefully so that what I had said was the truth, and yet I was not feeling good about returning there once more.

As we arrived back at the stately building that was now my home, my heart felt heavy and I had a sinking feeling, a feeling of disappointment. It felt that I was returning against my will and yet I was actually doing so of my own free choice. As I climbed those steep steps again up-to the front of Hawkstone Hall, I felt as if I was going to be there forever, that this was the only life for me. If this was what it was meant to be, surely then, this should not have been the way I felt? Surely I should be happy to return there?

Father Manson was there to welcome me back home. I think that he realised that I was in a fragile state of mind and that physically I was still not back to the person I was before I went into Hospital. He was quite fatherly in his approach, and he seemed to want me to ease back into the life quite slowly. He made no mention of our earlier telephone conversation and it seemed as if he was hoping that it would all go away and that I would just settle back into the normal Redemptorist way of life once more. It was good to see my friends again, the other brothers, although none of them were friends in the same way that I would have had in the outside world. There was always a distance between us, an aloofness, and they were friendly relationships, rather than relationships with friends. It was therefore impossible to confide in anybody, and with nobody to share my thoughts, fears and concerns, I would carry them all around with me like a huge burden. I sat in my cell again that evening. It was the first time I had been really alone since before I had gone into Hospital. I just stared at the blank walls and asked myself what I was doing back here? My thoughts again turned to my family. I had so much enjoyed their company once more and I wondered how long it would be before I saw any of them again. And then, Margaret came into my mind. After I had read her letter, in which she finished our relationship, I had deliberately tried to keep her out of my thoughts. Like her, I did not want Margaret to be the reason why I would leave the seminary. There had to be more deep seated reasons as well. But perhaps I had to accept that she was indeed one of the main reasons why I could not continue here. She was extremely kind, so understanding and very loving. It was a meeting of hearts and minds which I had never experienced before in my young life and I wondered if I could ever live a life without such an experience again. I gazed around the bare walls of my cell once more, and I felt trapped in a room, I felt trapped in a situation that I was struggling to control and I could see no end to it. Suddenly, the bell tolled! It was calling us to evening meditation. I awoke as if from a long daze and suddenly realised where I was. I was still in my civvies and had not changed into my Redemptorist garb. In a panic, I swiftly put on my black habit and white collar, fastened my rosary beads onto my belt and glanced into the bedroom mirror. Until now, I had been different. I had been a layman for a while, I had tasted the outside world again, but now, bedecked in my Redemptorist robes, I was one of the communities once more. The difference was that I no longer felt that I belonged to the Redemptorists any longer; I felt more like an intruder. Hurriedly, I scurried down the corridors and into the chapel. By now, everyone else was in their pews and deep in meditation. I squeezed past two of my brothers and into the place that was mine. I knelt in the pew and put my head into my hands, my elbows resting on the seat in front of me. At this point I should have put my mind into meditation mode, yet all I could think about was what I was still doing there. I tried hard to concentrate my mind and ask God for help to make the right decision. Has God really called me to be a priest? Was it my destiny to become a Redemptorist Missionary? I stared all around me in the chapel searching desperately for some inspiration, for somebody or something to tell me what to do. If I was a chosen one, then why did I not know it any more? I had not deliberately set out to reject the call from God to become a priest. At that point an old saying from the Gospel came into my mind: It went: *"Many are called, but few are chosen!" [Matthew 22:14]* The interpretation of this from the Gospel is not always easy to understand. From my perspective, I initially believed that I had been called to serve God as his priest, but that God had then chosen his priests from the number that had been called and that I was no longer in that special group, no longer a chosen one. If I had been, then surely it would have felt right, I would have felt happy and contented in that decision and I would have known that I had been called to his service.

As I silently meditated, I looked around me at my fellow brothers. Many had been there for years, and many more were on the road to becoming a priest, a brother and a missionary. These were all people I thought I knew, but I was never close enough to them, to really know the truth. I just believed that they were happy, and was convinced that they had answered their calling and that they were not silently going through the same traumas that I was experiencing. For me, gone was that feeling of belonging! Gone was the pride and passion that had made me want to become a Redemptorist. No longer was I excited to know that I would become a missionary and a Redemptorist Priest. Although I had kept an open mind and tried hard to succeed, I could no longer envisage that I could spend a lifetime in this solitary manner. That night, as I lay in my bed, I did not sleep well at all. There was too much swirling around in my head. From time to time, I would think again of Margaret and I would wish that I could be with her again. Yet the more I thought about it, the more I was convinced that Margaret was not the reason for me wanting to leave the Order. All the reasons had been there long before I entered Hospital, and those same reasons persisted after she had ended our relationship. It made me feel more at ease that I had come to this conclusion. Margaret had ended our relationship because she did not want to be the sole reason for me leaving, and indeed she was not. It was ironic then, that she only found out about it long afterwards and when it was all too late.

Over the next number of days, I did everything in my

power to lead as normal a life as I could. I did all the things that I usually did before, and I tried to knuckle down to my studies and throw myself into all the activities of the seminary. Fr Manson had asked me to come back to the seminary and to try as hard as I could to integrate back into the normal life. I knew that I owed it to him, my family and everybody else, including myself, to do just that and I did so with as much effort as I possibly could. For the next ten weeks I threw myself into everything that was going on at Hawkstone. I tried to concentrate on my studies during the classes and also during the evening sessions in my cell. I involved myself in as much as I was able. I did light work in the garden and went back to doing my catechism classes with the children in Shawbury. Father Manson thought that this would be good for me. I think that in my sub-conscious I was trying to keep my body active and busy all of the time so that I would not be able to think about the major issues that had to be resolved. For a long period, I did not even allow any thoughts of Margaret to linger on my mind. This was a good thing, because I now felt even surer, that meeting her was not the cause for me wanting to leave. Whereas I could have lived with that, I knew that Margaret could not, and so I was greatly relieved on that score.

During meditation sessions, or while out in the gardens on a walk, I would allow myself the luxury of thinking again about my situation. I had been trying to shut everything out of my mind and just concentrate on what I was doing at the time. On one occasion, as was my want, I walked alone in the outer grounds of Hawkstone Hall and climbed to the very top of the Monument. It was over 150 feet high and gave me a wonderful feeling of total isolation. It was a beautiful crisp and clear day and I could see for miles around. I had a lovely feeling which came from inside of me, a one-ness with nature, and a feeling of wonderful freedom, stood at the top and looking out. I did not want that moment to end. For the first time in a long time, in that moment, I actually felt good, but it was not to last. Once I had descended the steps to the bottom and had walked back in sight of the Hall I began once more to get feelings of being constricted, of being in a place where I no longer wanted to be. Slowly my dark clouds descended again, and my thoughts turned to negativity. I could not just keep pretending that all was well with the world. I could not lead the rest of my life feeling so unhappy and downhearted. I would have to do something about it.

A couple of days later, I had a chance conversation with one of the Brothers. It was to put an entirely different perspective on my thinking. On one of our post dinner afternoon walks in the garden, I teamed up with Brother Edmond. He was not an old man, perhaps in his early fifties, but he had been with the Order for around twenty five years. He was asking me about my time at Perth and Erdington. The conversation came around to some of my friends and Brothers that had left the Order during my time there. I told him how unhappy it had made me feel, when my good friends left. He told me that he was certain that there was absolutely no point in anybody staying with the Order unless they felt content and at peace with life at the Monastery. He said that there was no sense in anybody staying out of a sense of loyalty or duty. *"There is more than one way to lead a good life"* he said to me: *"Being a monk or a priest is not for everybody"*. He looked directly at me as he spoke the words. I felt as if he was aiming his remarks directly at me, even though I had never told him how I felt. It was as if he knew. Perhaps he could sense the unhappiness in my demeanour. His remarks had struck a chord with me and it was to leave a lasting effect. From that moment on, I knew exactly what I must do. My mind was made up. I was going to see Father Manson and tell him that my future lay outside of the Redemptorists. However, making my mind up and actually doing the deed were two separate issues. For the next two or three days I wandered around in something of a daze, going through the motions, the routine of daily life, but my mind and heart were not there any more. I really did feel like an outsider, and that I did not belong there anymore. It was about ten weeks since I had returned to Hawkstone, and I had tried and tried, but after that conversation with Brother Edmond, I knew that I must leave. I was very nervous, and I must have walked past his door on at least five or more occasions. Finally I stopped in front of Father Manson's cell, paused for several seconds and with my pulse racing, I knocked loudly three times: *"Come!"* came the reply: I walked into his cell and stopped by his desk: *"Father, I need to speak to you!"* I said, with emotion in my voice: *"Yes, I've been expecting you Brother. You had better sit down"*. I sat and looked at him, but the words did want to come out. *"Well, what do you want to talk about Brother?"* he said calmly: Quietly and slowly I replied: *"I am going to leave the Order Father, I want to start a new life outside. I have tried so hard, but I cannot be happy here any longer"*. There was a long silence before he said with a smile of resignation: *"Yes, Brother,*

I've been expecting it. I knew that you waned to leave. Life has been a struggle for you this year, hasn't it?"

As soon as I heard those words, it was as if a huge burden had been lifted from my shoulders and I could breathe easily once more. Father Manson advised me that I would need to have a dispensation of my vows from the Principle of the Redemptorist Order and he arranged that I would leave Hawkstone a few days later once that had been arranged. In the meantime I had the unenviable task of informing my parents. Of all the things I did not want to do, it was to tell my Mum and Dad that I would be leaving Hawkstone and that I would not become a priest. They have given up so much to help me get there and more than anything, there was the feeling that I had let them down and disappointed them that prayed on my mind. I knew how much it would hurt them, and as I told them down the telephone I could feel the disappointment in their voices. Mum had asked me what I would do from then on. The truth was that I had no idea whatsoever. Among all this, I had not even considered what I would do for my future. It seemed irrelevant at that moment, but for a start I had arranged to go and live back at home with my family at Marple where I would be able to rebuild my life again.

The next couple of days were strangely surreal. I continued to live in just the same way as I had done before and I was a finding it hard to envisage how life would be when I was not a Redemptorist any more. I had pangs of guilt and worries that I had made such a momentous decision even though I thought it was the correct one. I wondered if the past ten years been a complete waste of time. I did not tell anyone that I was shortly to leave as I did not have anyone who was that close that I felt I needed to. I just kept it all to myself and continued on as normal.

That afternoon I went into the chapel and prayed. I told God that I was sorry, but I did not believe that he wanted me as his priest, but I asked for his guidance for the rest of my life. I think I must have been hoping for a response of some kind from up above. It could have been anything, a bolt of lightening, a thunder clap or even just a feeling that I had been heard and understood. Of course, nothing was forthcoming, it rarely works that way, but at least I had a feeling inside of me that someone was listening to me.

Later, I took a walk around the grounds on my own. This was probably the last time I would do so, as the next day I would be leaving for the last time. To say that the walk was nostalgic was a gross understatement. I had spent so much time wandering the Hawkstone grounds that I must have known every nook and cranny inside it. Considering the fact that I was desperate to leave, I also had the most unusual feelings of sadness and sorrow, that I would be leaving the Redemptorists, Brothers, Priests, Hawkstone, Perth and Erdington, all of whom and which, had been a part of my childhood and now well into my manhood. I felt like some kind of addict, knowing that my addiction was not good for me, but that neither could I let it go.

Whilst I was fearful of life had I stayed, I was also even more afraid of leaving and stepping out alone into the big wide world. After all, this life with the Redemptorists, my adopted family, was the only life I had known since being a young eleven year old boy. I had done none of the things that normal young lads do. I had not had exciting teenage years like others had, bonding with the lads, going out with the girls, and at 22 yrs old, I had no experience of work, handling money, finance, or relationships.

That evening was nostalgic. At meditation and afterwards at supper, I looked around at all the people that had been a close part of my life for so many years. Some I had been with since I was eleven, others were more recent, but when living in such a community, in close proximity, I was unsure how I would live without them, even though I had no close relationships with any of them at all.

When I returned to my cell to sleep, it struck me that the next night I would not be in my cell; I would be in my bedroom at home in Marple. I would be with my birth family, in an entirely different way of life. I should have felt comforted, but instead I felt uneasy, unsure of what lay ahead, and that night it felt as if it was my life at Hawkstone that seemed like the safe haven, a place of familiarity. After all, it was what I had always known, and now it was my new life that was making me feel nervous of the future. It was strange how things had turned around. When I awoke the following day, I still had the same misgivings. I had lost my confidence in the decision I had made. I began to be fearful of going ahead and for a few minutes I wondered if I should go and tell Father Manson that it was all a big mistake and that I wanted to stay after all. Soon after, the bell tolled, and force of habit, I knelt by the side of my bed and prayed. This time I prayed that I had made the right decision and I asked God to somehow let me know if indeed he wanted me to stay. Again, I did not expect a reply from above, but in a strange way I wanted him to let me know, somehow and by any means, if he wanted me to stay after all, but nothing was to happen. Quickly, I got to my feet, washed and shaved, and put my Redemptorist Habit on. I glanced into the mirror on my door, to check that everything was straight. Immediately, the image staring back at me caused me to question who and what I was. From my first day as a Novice I had always been proud to wear my habit. It made me feel like somebody quite special. It immediately transformed me from plain old Stephen Nearey into *"Stephen Nearey CSSR, Redemptorist."* It gave me that feeling of pride in who I was, who I was representing and like any uniform, [a policeman, a nurse or a pilot,] it gives the wearer that pride and confidence in the organisation, and a pride and confidence in ones self. I realised as I stared into the mirror in my cell that this would be the last time I would wear that uniform, and it gave me pangs of sadness and a degree of regret. Pulling myself together again, I hurried down to morning meditation. I probably prayed more intensely during that session than I had ever done in my life. The realization of leaving was hitting home and despite knowing inwardly that it was the right thing to do, I could not but help my feelings of some regret and sorrow. I prayed again that I had made the correct decision and for help in the next stage of my life whatever that might be. My belief in God, at that stage, was as strong as it had ever been, but I also now believed that God had not chosen me to be a priest, otherwise I would have felt right, and had the strength and resolve to carry it through to its final completion.

Breakfast as always, was taken in silence. It was just as well because it would have been awkward and difficult to talk to my Brothers, knowing that I would be leaving in just a few short hours. With hind-sight I should have told some of them that I was leaving. After all, I had lived with many of them for several years and was as close with them as anybody was permitted to be in the Redemptorist Order. Perhaps some already knew, but it was not spoken about, and I would leave without telling anybody about it.
Since returning to Hawkstone I had been put on extra rations in order to build me up after my stay in Hospital. I had lost a lot of weight and was still very thin and somewhat gaunt looking. I finished my cereal and had extra portions of poached eggs and toast in order to help me gain some weight. This was to be my last meal and the closer the time came to leaving, the sadder and more withdrawn I became. After Breakfast I would normally go out and do my morning job. Each of the students was allocated a household job so that Hawkstone Hall was spick and span by 10am each day. Before I went into Hospital I had been given the job of cleaning several of the corridors each morning. While I was away for six weeks, this was done by another Brother, and so I went straight to my cell. Father Manson had arranged for me to be taken home later that morning and I awaited his call. I did not want to walk around the Hall as I felt awkward in engaging in conversation with anybody. I would have found it difficult to tell them, to explain why I was leaving and just how I felt. More than anything, I had a feeling of failure and of letting people down. All of these years I had spent with the Redemptorists, and now it had come to nothing. I felt sorry for the people who had invested so

much time and effort in me, and I felt so sorry for myself.
I was sat in my cell, just thinking, and gazing around the room. There was not much to see. I had emptied my sparse personal belongings from my cupboards and drawers and had put them into a hold all. They didn't amount to much after ten years, just a few clothes, a St. Christopher chain and a few nick knacks was all that it amounted to. But that was what a vow of poverty was all about and I had wanted for nothing during my time there.
At eleven o'clock there was a knock on my door. It was Brother John. He told me that Father Manson would like to see me in his rooms. Without any conversation, I went along the corridors and knocked on his door. *"Come,"* was his reply! *"Brother Nearey, please sit down"* he said in his calm bland voice. *"I am very sorry to see you leave, but I think it will be for the best. You are clearly not happy here, and have not been for some time. I know you have tried very hard and I will miss you very much as will all the Brothers here".* I found it hard to reply and I felt choked, but I said: *"Thank you Father, I have tried so hard to make it work, but I cannot be happy here. It is not for me, so I have to go".* At that, Father Manson said that there were a few matters to sort out. He pulled out a document and told me that he had a letter to me from the General Superior of the Redemptorists in London which dispensed me from my vows of poverty, chastity and obedience. He asked me to sign the letter and then he gave me a copy of the letter from the General Superior. It was written entirely in Latin, the language of the Catholic Church. I had studied Latin since the age of twelve, and so I had no difficulty in understanding the words that had been put in front of me. It stated in simple but clear terms

that I had been relieved of my vows and that made me free to follow a normal life outside of the Church. I signed the papers that Father Manson had put in front of me, and from that moment I was a layman again. I cannot say that I felt happy or even relieved that this had happened. In effect, it was the equivalent of being divorced. After all, I had been married to the Church, and now it had been dissolved. For me, there was just a felling of flatness, of sadness that, like a marriage, it had just not worked out. I only felt pleased that the parting of the ways was on good terms. I was sad to be leaving and they were unhappy to see me go. I would always have a deep love and respect for the Redemptorists and the people who I had shared my life with, all those years. Father Manson was nothing but practical. He had thought of all the things that had to be done, while none of it had occurred to me. He told me I would need some money to get me started in my new life, and he handed me an envelope with £20. It was not a lot, even in 1970, but it was enough to help me to start my new life. He then told me that Brother John would drive me home and that he would tell all my fellow Brothers about my leaving, during lunch. He added that they would all pray for me that day, that I would be happy in my new life. Finally he asked me to just leave my habit in my cell. He said that they would alter it for one of the Novices next year. At that, he gave me his blessing and a firm shake of his hand and said to me: *"Bless You, Be Happy, Stephen."* At that exact moment I felt just like a child that had pestered his parents for a treat, but as soon as his wish had been granted, he realised that he did not want it after all. As I walked from his chambers, my first thought was that my Redemptorist life had come to an abrupt end, as indeed it had. Suddenly I was a layman again. I did not belong at Hawkstone anymore and yet I had no future mapped out for me anywhere else. I was back in "No Man's Land" once again, having been cut off from going back in the direction I had just travelled, but not knowing which direction to head for next. I stood in the corridor for several seconds outside Father Minson's door not quite knowing what to do next. My first inclination was to go back to my cell, but next I felt a pressing need to go outside. I felt the call for wide open spaces and fresh air. As soon as I reached the outside door, I instinctively headed up the hill at the front of Hawkstone Hall and straight towards the Monument. I walked there faster than I had ever done so before, still in my Redemptorist habit. Instinctively, my mind was telling me that my days were numbered and even the hours and minutes were running out. I reached the foot of the "Sir Rowland Hill Monument" and then I fairly ran up the one hundred and twelve spiralled steps until I reached the terrace around the summit. This had always been my place and I gazed all around the 360 degrees, marvelling at the beautiful countryside below and stretching out for many miles over the view that encompassed twelve counties. In my mind, I thought that I would never come to this place again, and that thought filled me with sadness. Realising that time was short I wanted to go one last time to all the places that had meant so much to me over the past three years. Hurriedly, I scampered down the spiral stone steps picking up the hem of my habit so as not to trip in my haste to see all my favourite places for one last time. My next stop was at the Grotto, the dark and dismal caves that I had frequented so often. On exiting the Grotto, I marvelled at the sandstone rocks, high up, in which they had been carved. The views over the land and the Golf Course were simply magnificent. When that was done, I went in haste back towards the Hall and briskly walked around the rear of the building to my favourite gardens where I had been the "Lawn maker". The next stop was to the man made lake that I and my fellow brothers had painstakingly dug out and then landscaped. I stood there for a few moments thinking of the hard work and fun we had in creating this masterpiece. Realising that time was short, I wondered into the walled vegetable gardens where I had spent time chatting to the Brothers who cultivated it and grew the produce for our table. Then finally I wandered slowly up and along the single line of graves in the cemetery where so many of our fellow Brothers had been laid to rest. I glanced at the time on the Church Clock. I did not have my own watch. I now knew that my time was short, and that finally, my time here was done. I meandered back into Hawkstone Hall via the chapel. I went in for one last time and instead of kneeling, I just sat in the pew in the back row and quietly said a prayer that I had done the right thing. Nothing came into my head to suggest that it was the wrong decision and so I left. I walked back through the cloisters to my cell in a complete daze. I thought I should feel happy at this point and yet I felt just the opposite. I stood in my cell, my bag was packed, and I put my dispensation papers and the envelope containing the money, into the bag. I glanced into the mirror one last time to check that everything was done. I still had my habit on and I had forgotten all about it! It had become such a part of me over the past four years that I felt strange without it. Slowly I took it off and carefully I put it onto a hanger and hung it on the back of my door. Instead, I put on my black suit and plain white shirt, but instead of the "dog" collar by which priests and religious people are recognised, I just left my shirt collar open. I did have a black tie, but it all seemed a little formal. I didn't really have any other clothes except for a black sweater. The rest were outside work clothes which I left behind. Finally, it was all done. I took one final glance around the cell that had been home for three years, and then fondly looked out of the window at the cultured lawns that had been my responsibility to maintain. They looked beautiful, and with no mole hills! As I was admiring my work, there was a tap on my cell door, and there stood Brother John, his usual smile on his face, and he just said to me: *"Taxi to Marple, Stephen"*. As I wandered down the cloister behind Brother John, my suitcase in my hand, I gazed at the Monastery one final time. I passed by the beautiful public rooms, the library and the ballroom and the thought came into my head that I may never see them again. Although I had to do it, I had to leave, I had pangs of loss and found it difficult to let go. In a moment, my mind also flashed back to my six years as a boy at Erdington and my year as a Novice at Perth, not to mention the three years I had just finished at Hawkstone. At the time it felt like they were "lost years", a wasted passage of time in my life, and now it had all come to an end. There may well have been a new life ahead of me, just waiting to be lived, but I had no idea what it would entail, where I was going and what would I do. As I mused over the possibilities, I felt fretful and unsure. I climbed into the car, gave one more furtive glance over my shoulder at Hawkstone Hall and then left

Twenty

The Final Solution

Brother John knew the score. In fact, I think that he had been aware from our conversation on the last journey from Marple to Hawkstone, that all was not well. It was not that I had spoken a lot, or said anything in particular; it was perhaps my body language that told the tale. At first I was quiet on the journey home. It was a lot to take in. I had just made a massive life changing decision and I was full of uncertainty and insecurity. All I knew was that I was going back home, to start a brand new life and that I had left Hawkstone for the final time. I just looked out of the car window at the passing countryside and my mind was a blank. There was no point in reflecting any more on the Redemptorist Life. It was now all in the past, albeit I would take with me, a huge number, of good and not so good memories of my time there. As we drove along, Brother John tried to lift the mood: With a glint in his eye he said: *"Come on Steve, Cheer up! You've just left the Mad House!"* I laughed, possibly for the first time in a long time. He said it to cheer me up. He carried on: *"You'll soon be home, you're a young man, and you want to stop looking backwards now and start to look forward again. You've got your whole life ahead of you. Live it!"*

As we reached my parent's home I invited Brother John into the house for a cup of tea to refresh him for the journey back to Hawkstone. He declined. He said: *"Just forget about Hawkstone now Stephen, you can think about it in many years to come. Just get on with your life and be Happy!"* I shook him by the hand, warmly and then spontaneously, gave him a strong hug. His wise words had set me onto a more positive line of thinking. He was a wise man indeed. I stopped to wave to him as he set off on the long drive back to Hawkstone. I then picked up my bag before heading for the front door at No.66, my home.

I wasn't exactly sure what kind of reception I would get at home. Of course I did receive a warm welcome, I was their son, and I was coming home, but I knew it would be a crushing blow for them. My parents had set their heart on me becoming a priest, and especially with the Redemptorist Order. I could feel the disappointment in their voices and the way they were with me at first. I felt as if I had let them down. They were the staunchest of Roman Catholics and it meant so much to them. I felt so very sorry for them, but it was my life and I had to lead it according to my own hopes, belief and convictions.

My first couple of weeks back home were extremely difficult. My old life had gone, but my new life had not got under "starters orders". I just needed a period of time in order to get my mind in order and to start re-building a new life for myself. My days were just so different. After the structured life at Hawkstone, my days at home were empty by comparison. I had no job, no money, barely any clothes and nothing to do in life. I had no interests, no hobbies, no clubs and I did not go to pubs. The transition to life in the outside world was going to take quite some time and effort in order for me to come to terms with it. In one of the quieter moment at home, of which there were many, I don't really know my reason for doing it, but I decided to write a letter to Margaret. In it, I told her that I had now left Hawkstone and that I was living with my parents back home in Marple. I told her that I had left the Seminary but I assured her that she was definitely not the reason for me making that decision. I just had to tell her the reasons why I had left, as I did not want her to feel in anyway responsible for me not continuing there. I did though add that in all honesty, my meeting her had helped me to clarify what it was in life that I wanted to do, and what was right for me. I just had to tell her the real truth.

I was not sure what kind of response, if any, that I would receive. I did not hear from Margaret for over a week and then I received a letter. It was with some anticipation that I opened it. In her letter, she told me that she was shocked to hear that I had left the Seminary. She said that she understood my reasons for leaving, but even so, she felt that meeting with her had been the cause of me making that decision and that she just could not cope with that knowledge and the ensuing guilt and pain it had caused.

She ended the letter by telling me that she had got back together with her old boyfriend Dave, and that they were trying to make a go of it together. She ended by saying that she wanted to remain friends and keep in touch with me. I was also shocked to hear Margaret's news, although I had no right to expect anything other than that. I must unwittingly, have caused her a great deal of heartache, and I was pleased that she seemed to be getting her life back together. In many ways, I felt vindicated that it was not Margaret that had been the cause of my decision to leave and I felt better for that. I did not reply to her letter right away. I thought it would be prudent to allow both of us to get our own lives back on track again, although I fully intended to contact her again, once the dust had settled and we both had some clarity of thought on our new lives.

Meantime, for the next few weeks, I just concentrated on building my new life. I was slowly coming around and I found that I was not thinking too much about my previous life at Hawkstone anymore. Instead, I was concentrating on life with my family and finding a job. Prospective employers were not exactly queuing up to employ a twenty two year old ex-Monk with no real skills except for Philosophy, Latin and the Classics. It was good though, to spend time with, not only my parents, but also with my two brothers and sister. It helped me greatly to settle into a new normality. I must confess that I did, from time to time, think about Margaret and what might have been, in different circumstances, but she was settled again with her ex boyfriend and I was pleased for her. I had it in my mind to write to her again, purely as a friend, and then perhaps to phone her for a chat. I had precious few friends. In fact, when I weighed up the situation, I had no friends at all. All the lads I may have called friends had left and were scattered all over the country, but I had no idea where. It really was a case of building a new life with new friends. In the meantime, Margaret was perhaps my only confidante, the only person that I could share my thoughts and concerns with, on just about anything. I decided that I would write to her again quite soon, but before I did so, a letter dropped on the mat. Immediately I recognised her lovely hand writing and the postmark.

I opened the letter in private, in my room. I was expecting a bubby and newsy letter telling me how she was going on. Instead it was a sad and serious letter from the start:

"My Dear Steve,
I told you that I had got back together with Dave. Well things were going very nicely between us and we had decided to get married and had set a date for the wedding. Three weeks ago, we were driving along a country road; Dave was driving, when a car pulled out of a side road and straight into our path. We were going quite fast and I yelled at Dave to brake, but it was too late. Dave was not wearing a seat belt and he went straight through the windscreen and was killed instantly. The funeral was last week. I have some injuries, but nothing too serious and I am alright. I am absolutely devastated. I cannot write any more, as I am too upset, but I will be in touch again once I feel more able"
All my love
Margaret XX

I just stared at the one page letter in sheer disbelief. It was all too much to take in. I felt so devastated for Margaret and I felt that I wanted to help her, but it did not seem appropriate. I don't know what I could have done anyway. Margaret had "lost" one person, [me] when our brief relationship had to come to an end, and then tragically, in just a matter of weeks, she had lost her fiancée, tragically killed just weeks before they were due to be married. It was a cruel twist of fate and one which she did not deserve. She was one of life's beautiful people. My own feelings paled into minute insignificance, in comparison to hers, but even so, I deeply felt Margaret's loss. I wanted to be with her, to support her in her time of need and to comfort her, but it did not feel right to do so, even though I was now a "free" man and able to do what I wanted. I did not know her family, or Dave's who had lost his life so suddenly and tragically. I was an outsider, in that respect, and my presence would not have been appropriate at that particular time. I would phone her and give her my love and support and then leave the families to grieve for a period of time, before I would make contact once more.

I should not have been so insensitive at a time like that, but the thought came into my mind that there could still possibly be a chance for me and Margaret once more. It may be sometime in the future, and after a respectful period of time, yet I did not know if it could happen again.

That night as I lay in bed, I was still shell-shocked. I pondered the events that had taken place since I had left the Monastery, and sadly, the news from Margaret that I had received earlier on that day. My mind was subconsciously analysing and dissecting the events that had taken place in my recent life, and then the following thoughts came clearly into my mind;

I very **Nearly** had a beautiful girl called Margaret, but I had loved and lost her, and we was destined not to be.

I very **Nearly**, after four years as a Redemptorist Monk, became a Missionary Priest, but it was destined not to be.

In all honesty, I really was just; **"The Nearly Man."**